Tiffany Toland-Scott's
Spellbinding Darkness

A selection of digital paintings
from 2008-2012

ISBN-13: 978-0615725680
ISBN-10: 0615725686

Tiffany Toland-Scott
Tiffany's Realm
PO BOX 254
EAST HELENA, MT 59635
UNITED STATES OF AMERICA

tiffany@epiphany.gallery

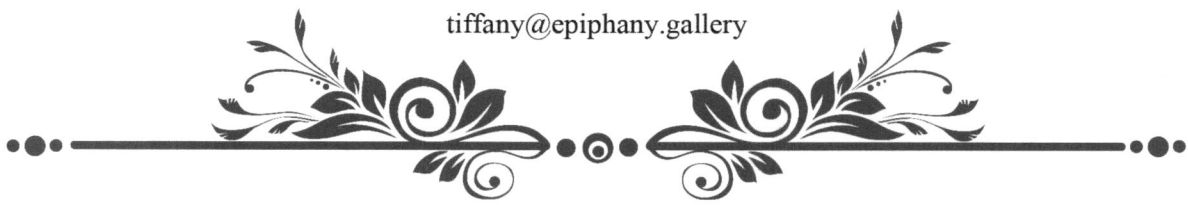

First Edition
First Printing, 2015

Introduction

In 2012 I started this adventure. My supporters had been asking for years for an art book, and I wanted to deliver. No stranger to self-publishing, I assumed this would be an easy task that I could undertake and complete in just a matter of days. It is now January of 2015 and this book is finally, hopefully, coming to fruition.

It's been an uphill battle, and many things have changed. This book leaves off at the end of 2012. I was still firmly a digital artist, creating each of my paintings one brush stroke at a time in programs like Photoshop and Painter. I had painted this way for several years, and did not imagine that I would stop any time soon.

As summer was breathing its last breaths in 2013, a new friend encouraged me to give oils a try. I had been giving acrylics a go, but not achieving what I knew I could achieve with paint. He understood my frustration and told me he had felt the same about acrylics, but oils had opened a new world of opportunity to him. In the end I found myself in an art supply store in Savannah, Georgia with a fist full of cash which I readily exchanged for a set of about twenty oil paints, some mediums, brushes, and other tools I thought I might need. I have never looked back since.

As much as I love digital art, and as much as I learned from creating it, there was always something missing for me. I wanted to touch the paintings, to feel the drag of the canvas beneath my brush. Instead, digital art left me always separated from my creations by a sheet of glass; the only sensory experience the drag and click-tapping of a stylus on a digital tablet.

In a way, this book almost feels like a "goodbye", or a memorial for a fondly-remembered friend. In other ways, it just feels like loose ends finally getting tied up. The truth is by the time oils came along the love was already gone.

So here it is, and here we go, off on another adventure. But, before I go, here is the book I promised nearly three years ago; a fond farewell to my training wheels.

Tiffany

Fallen

Dark angels, vampires, werewolves,
& wicked women

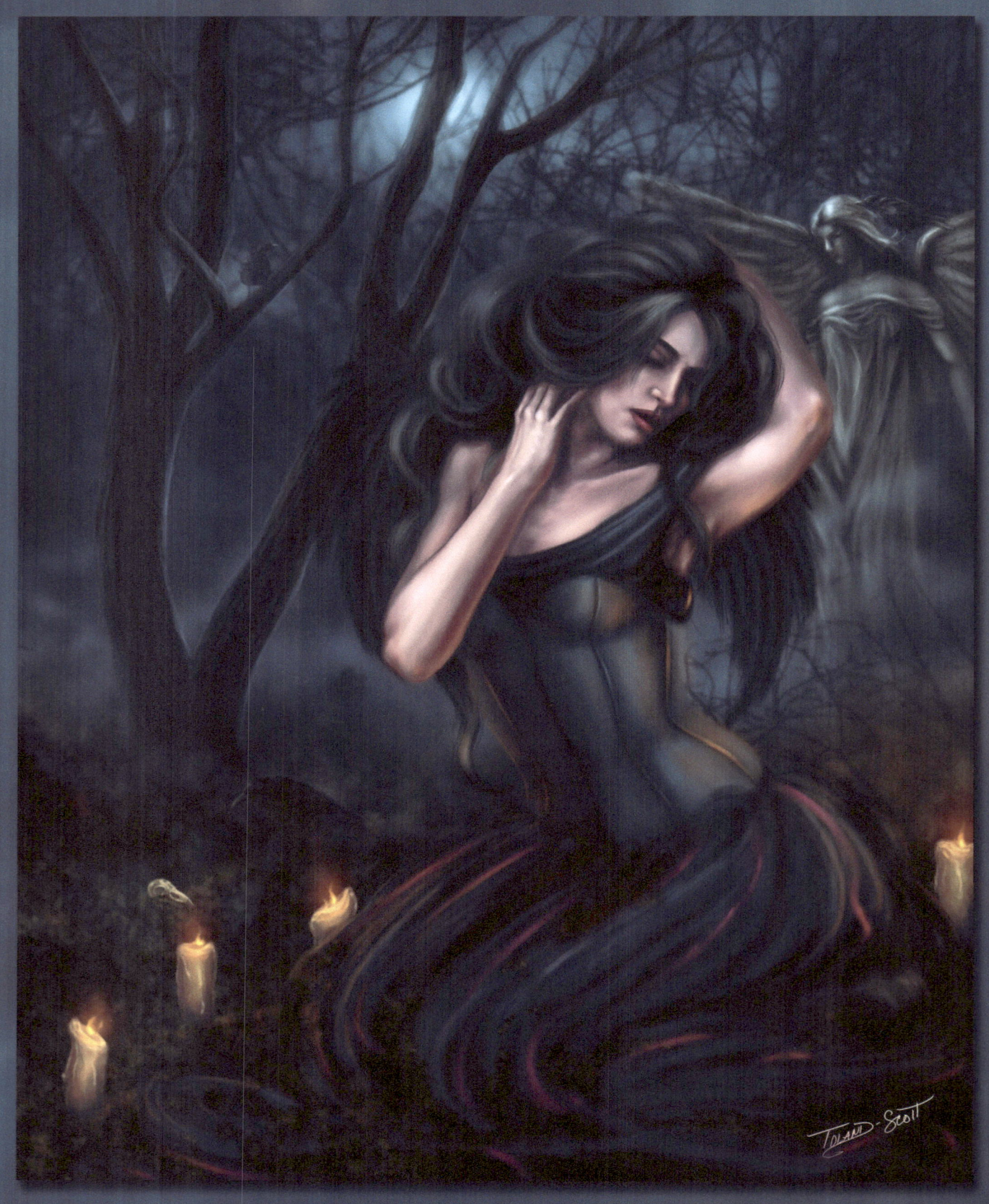

"Death", 2012

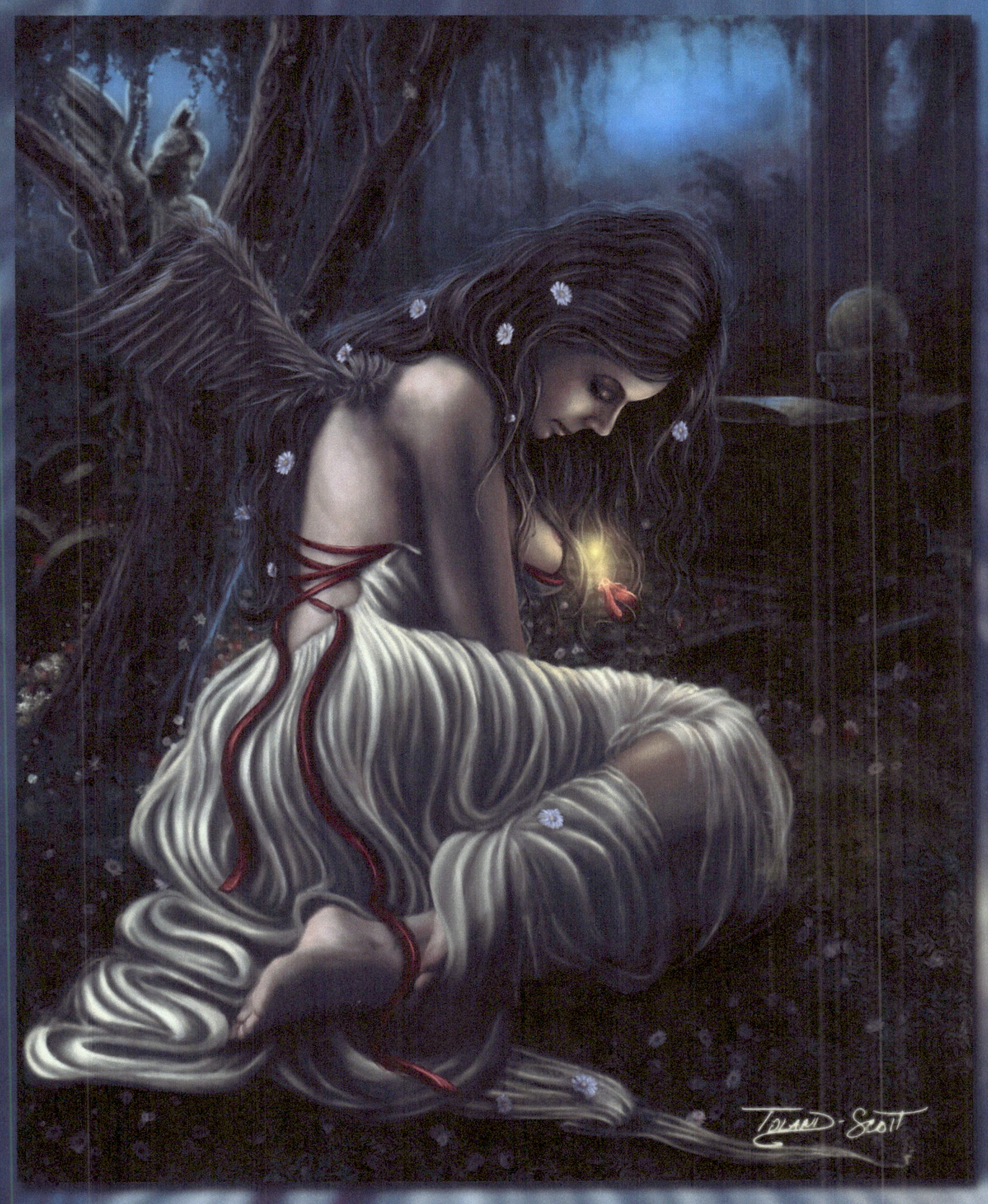

"Rebirth", 2012

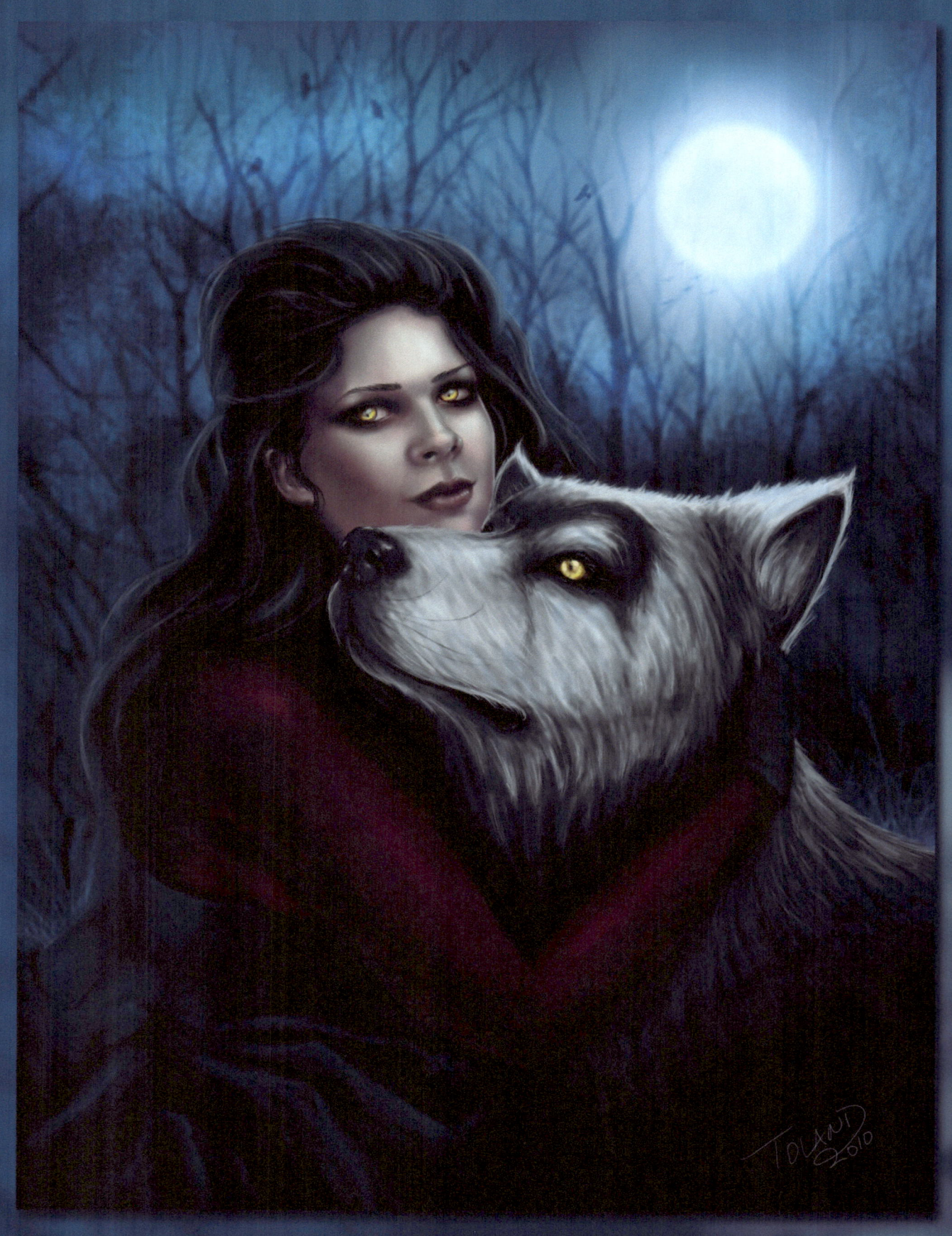

"Lupa", 2010

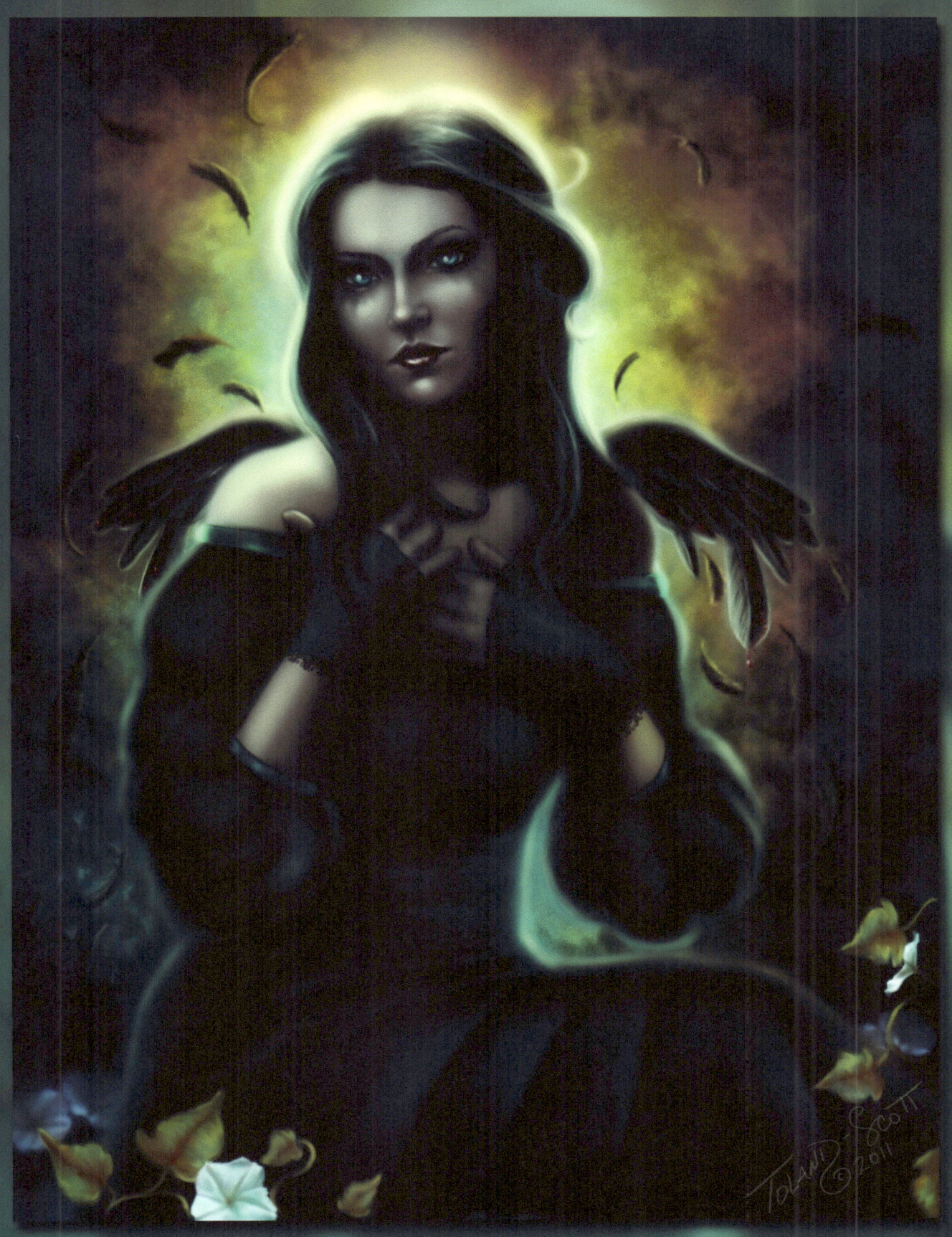

"Maldita", 2011

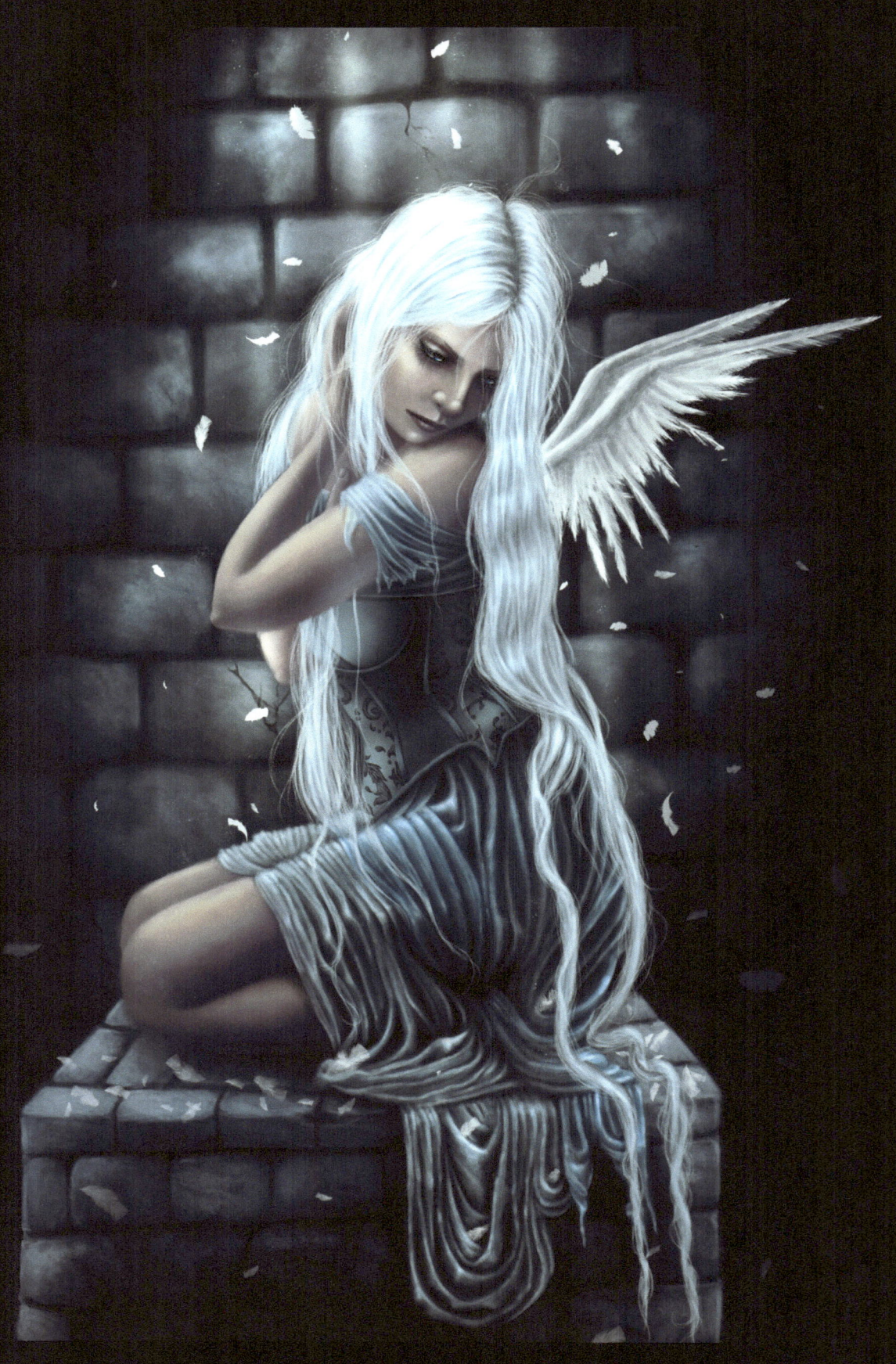

"Forgotten", 2008

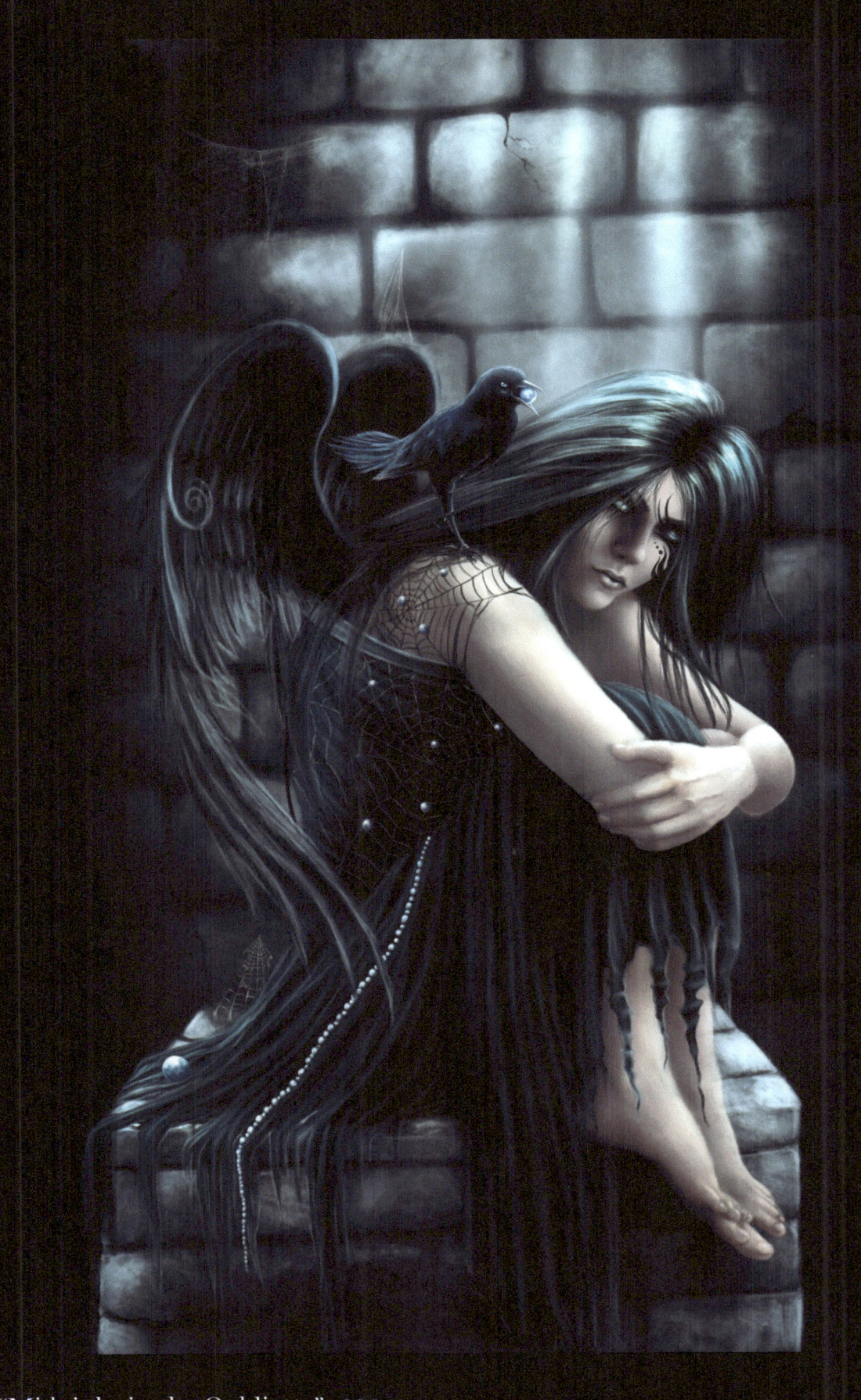

"Midnight in the Oubliette", 2008

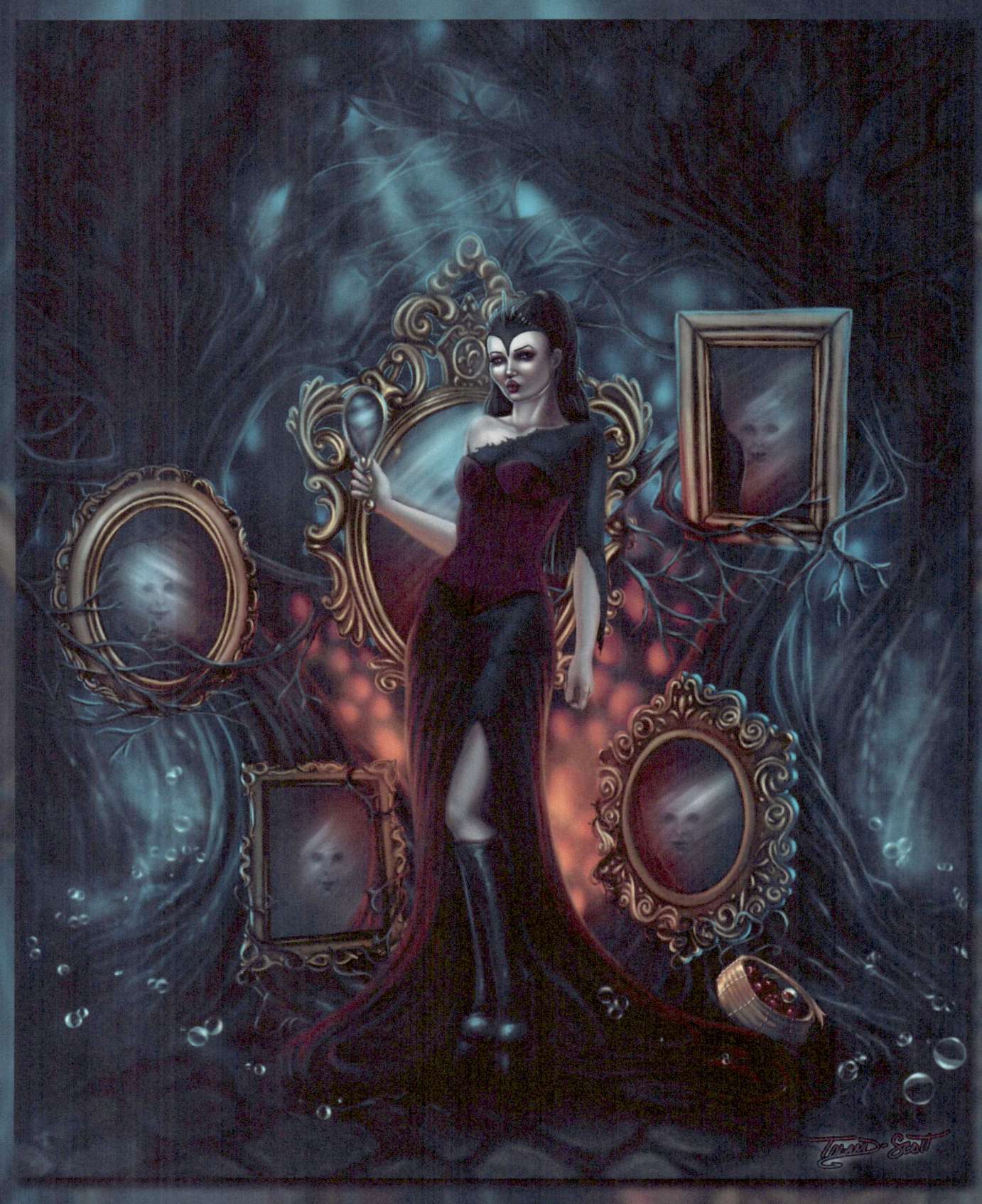

"Evil Queen Complex", 2012

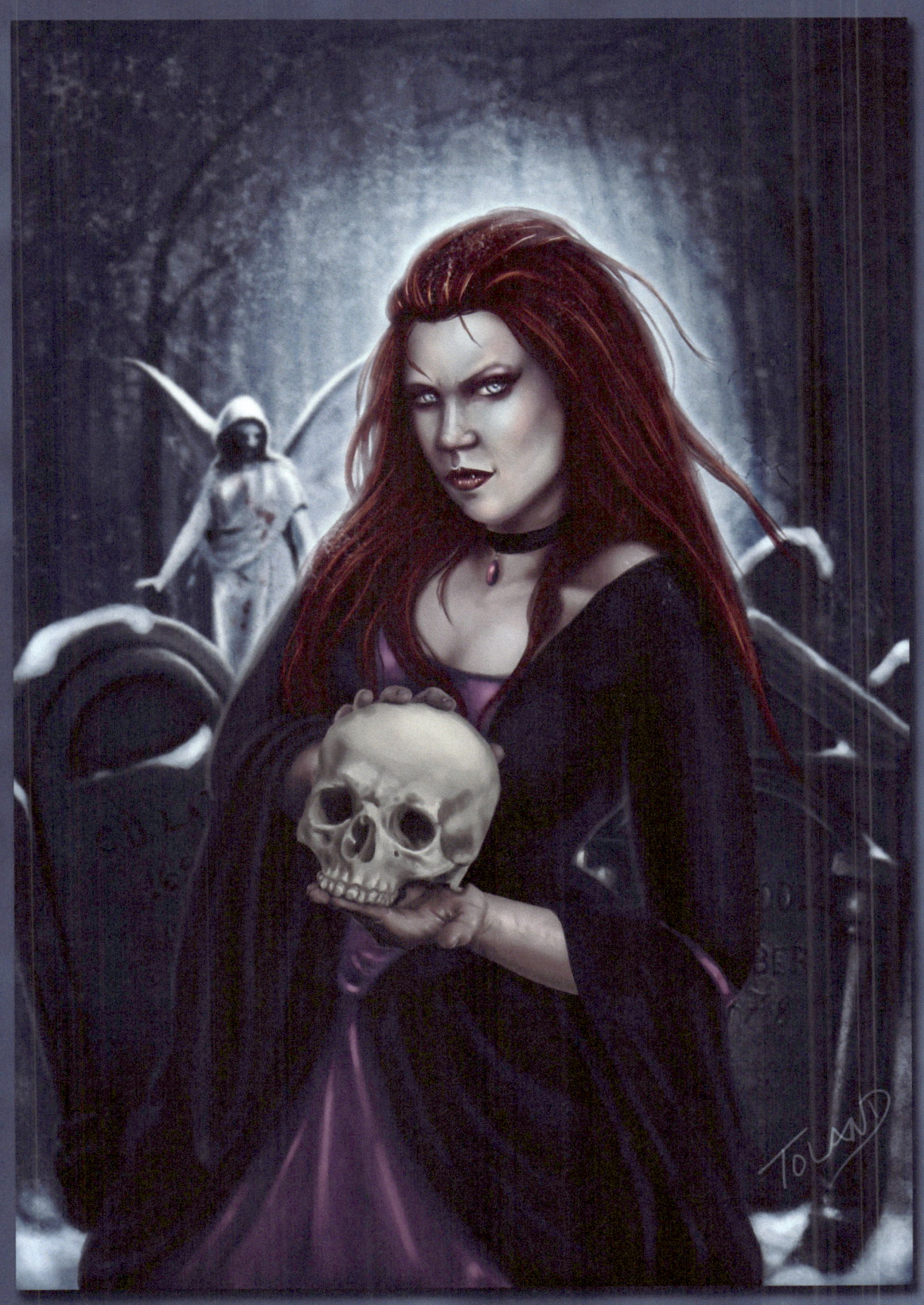

"A Warning", 2010

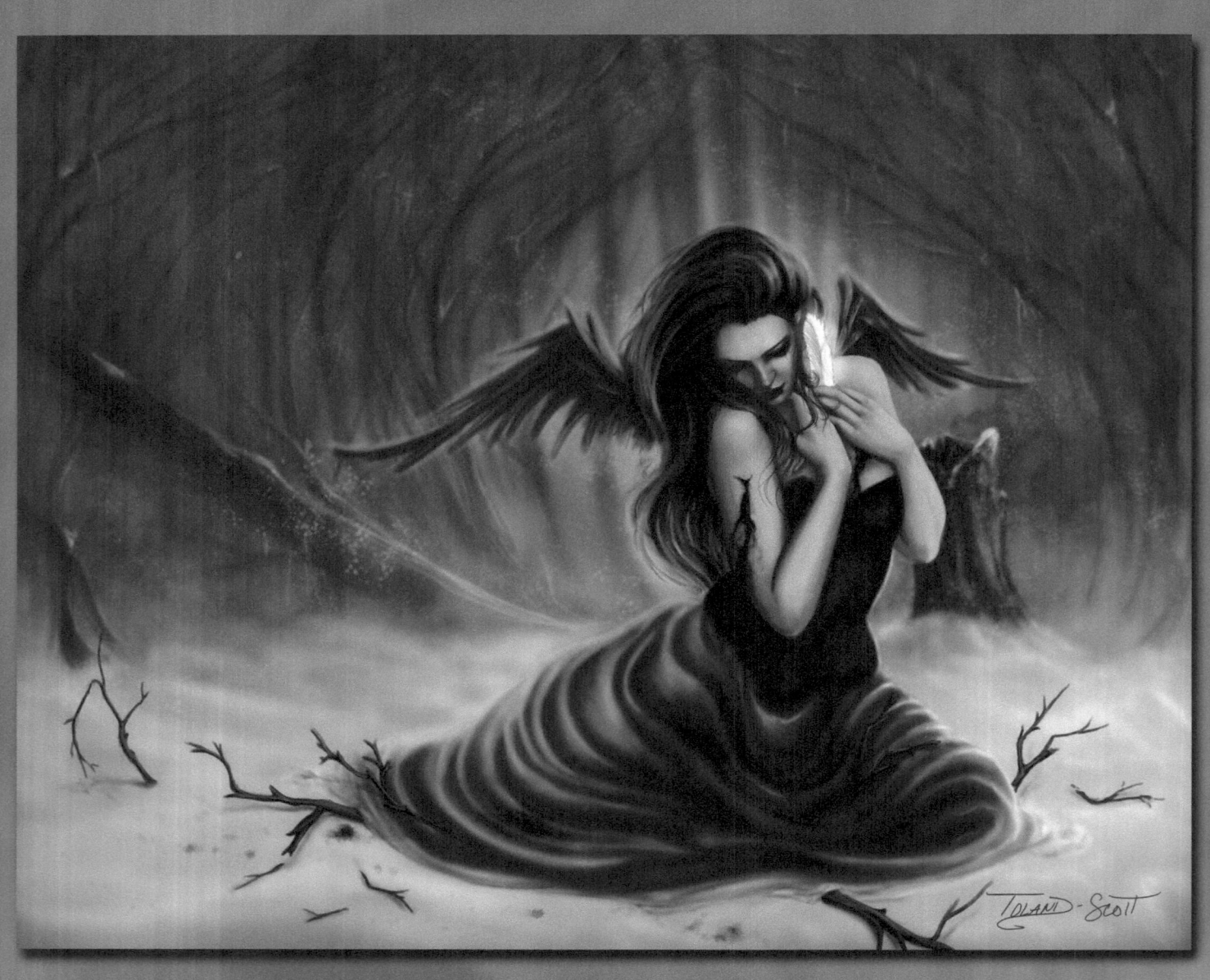

"Last of My Innocence", 2012

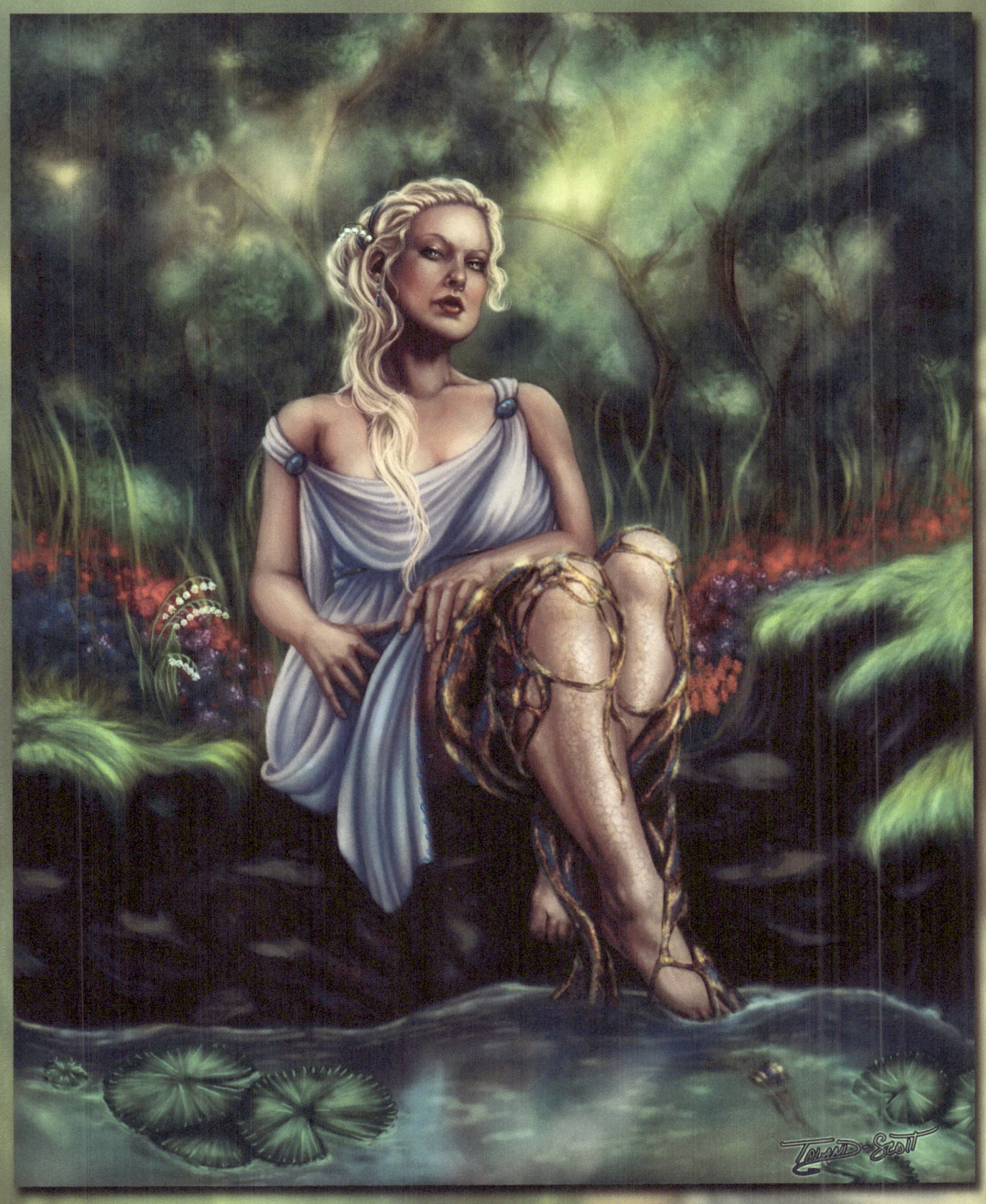

"Lamia", 2012

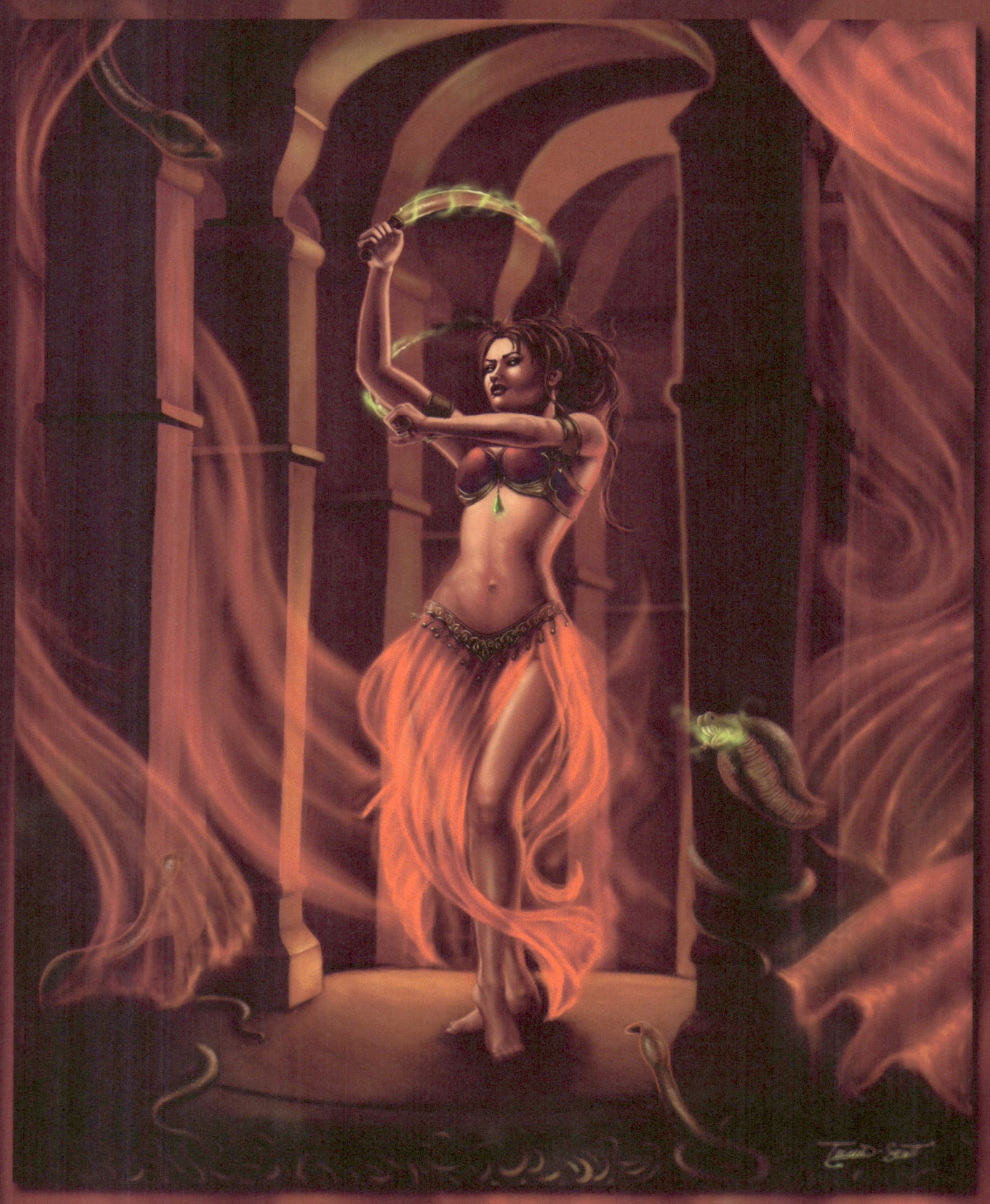

"Venom", 2012

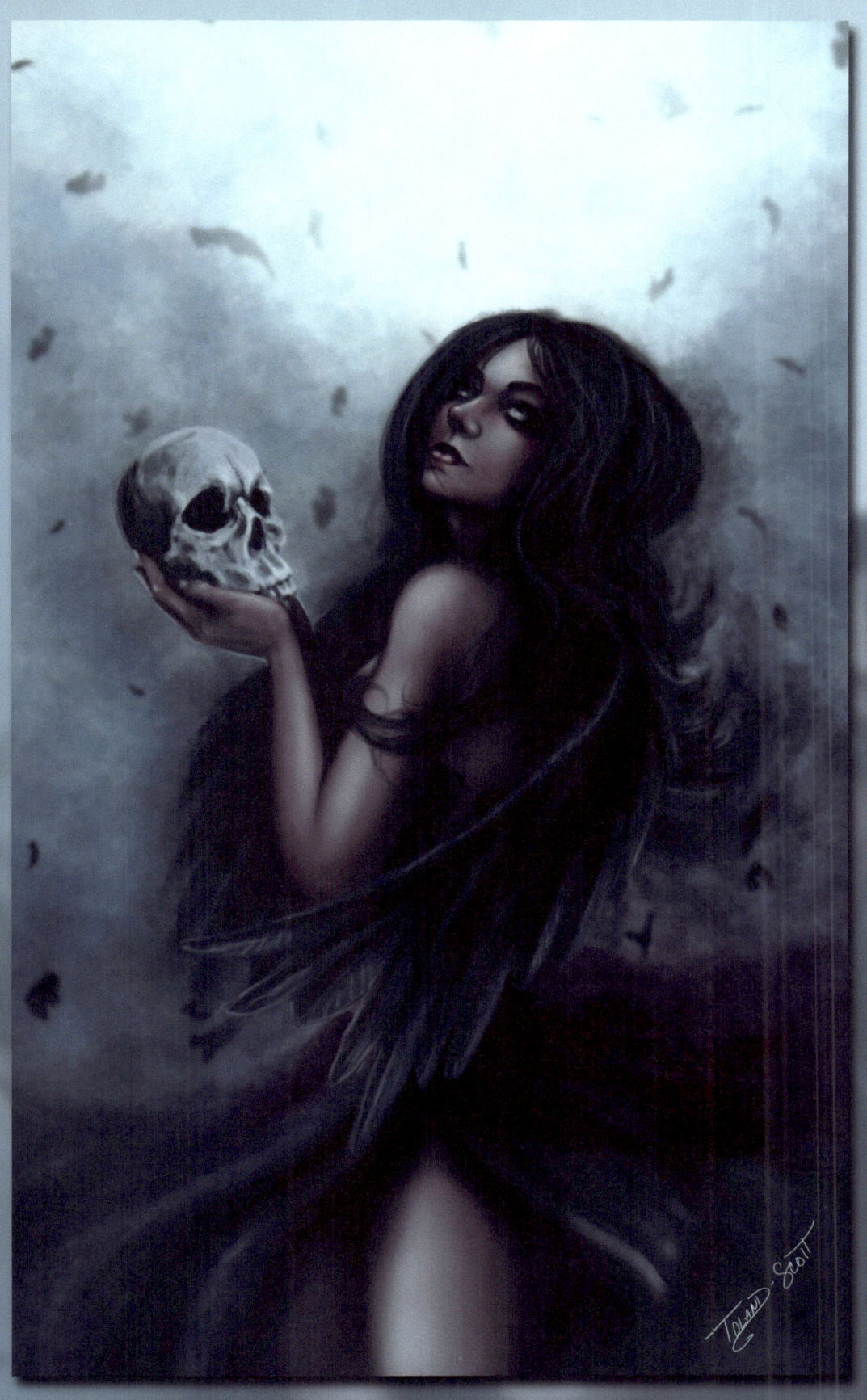

"Call of the Morrighan", 2012

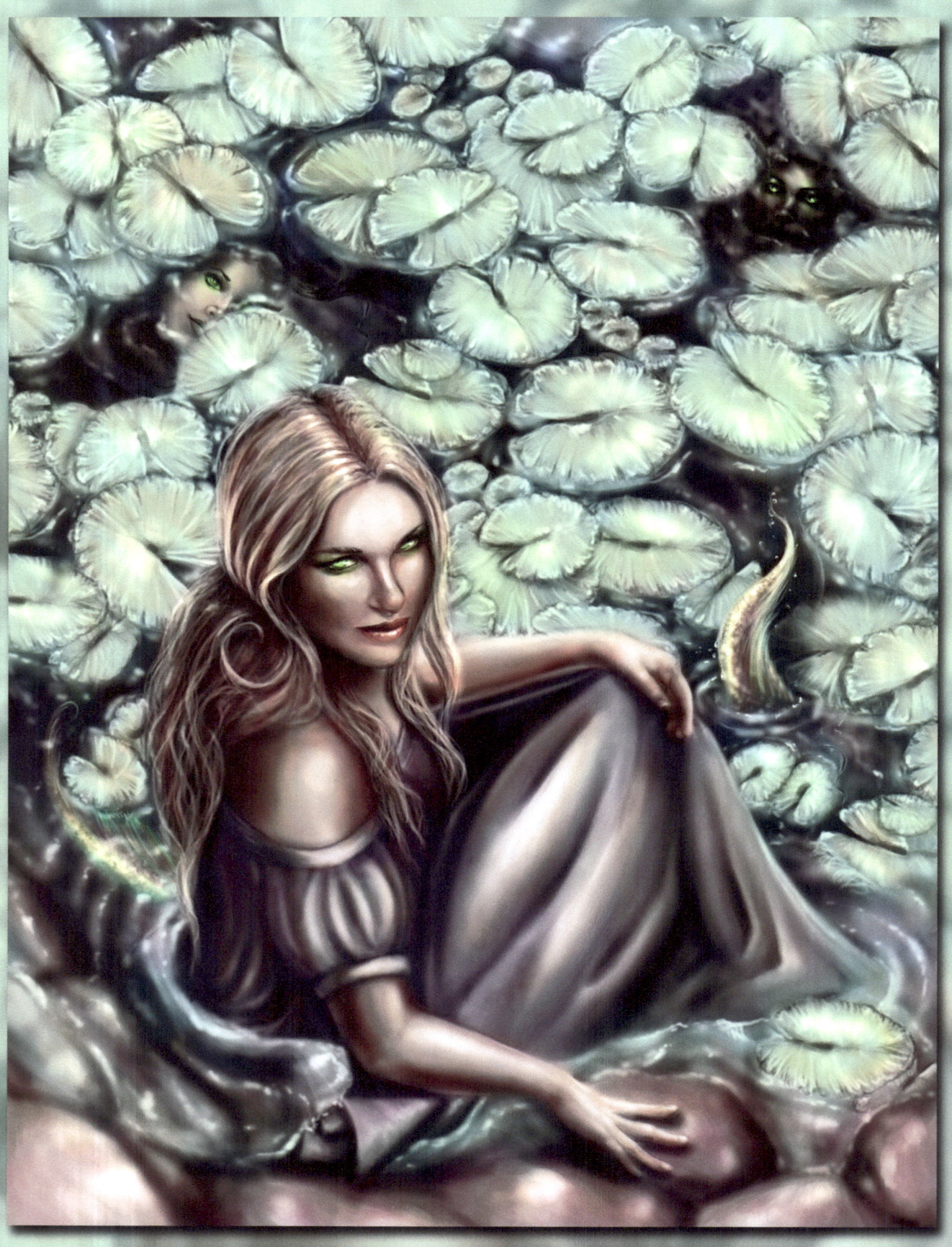

"Join Us?", 2010

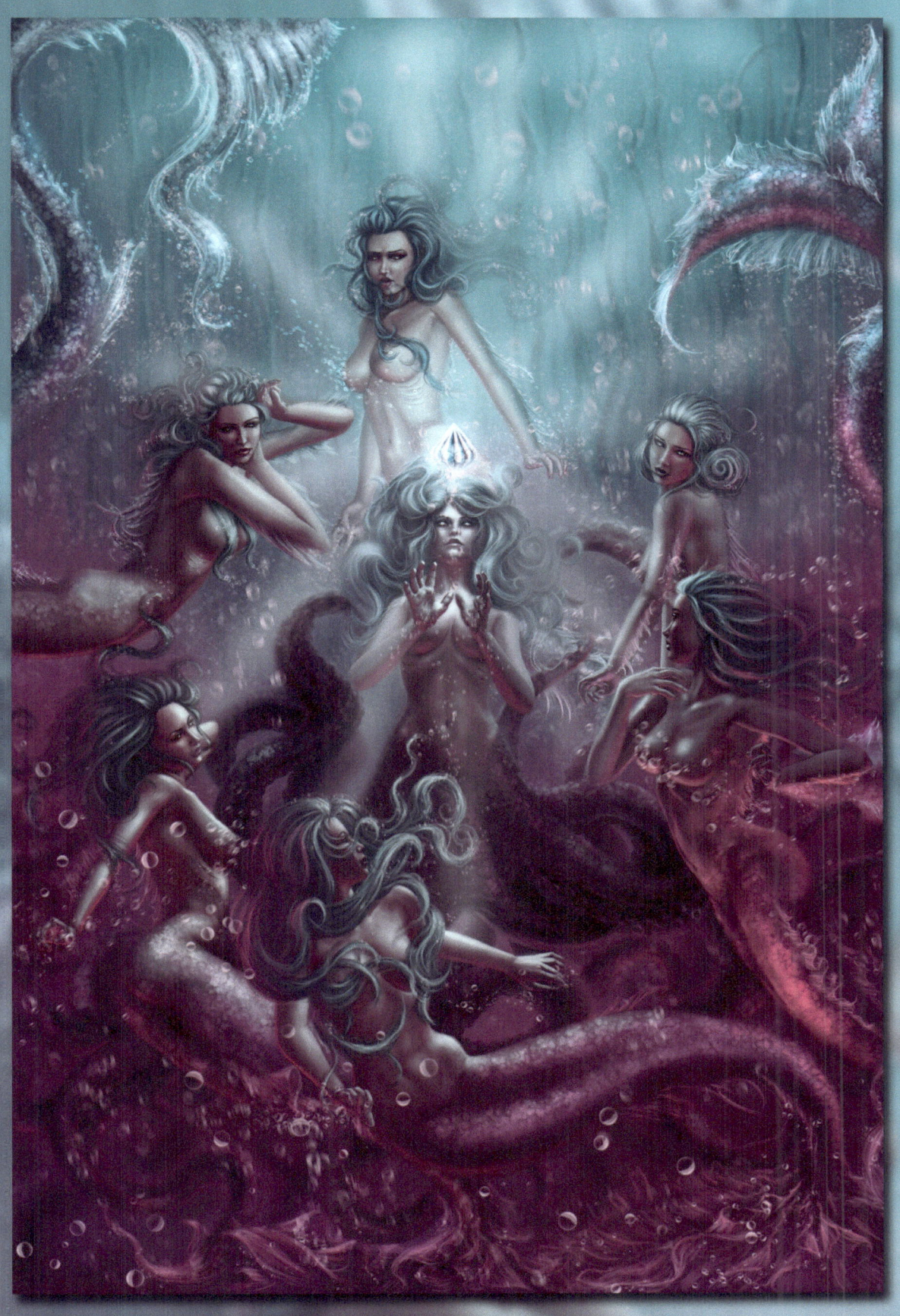

"Seven Sirens and the Silver Tear", 2012

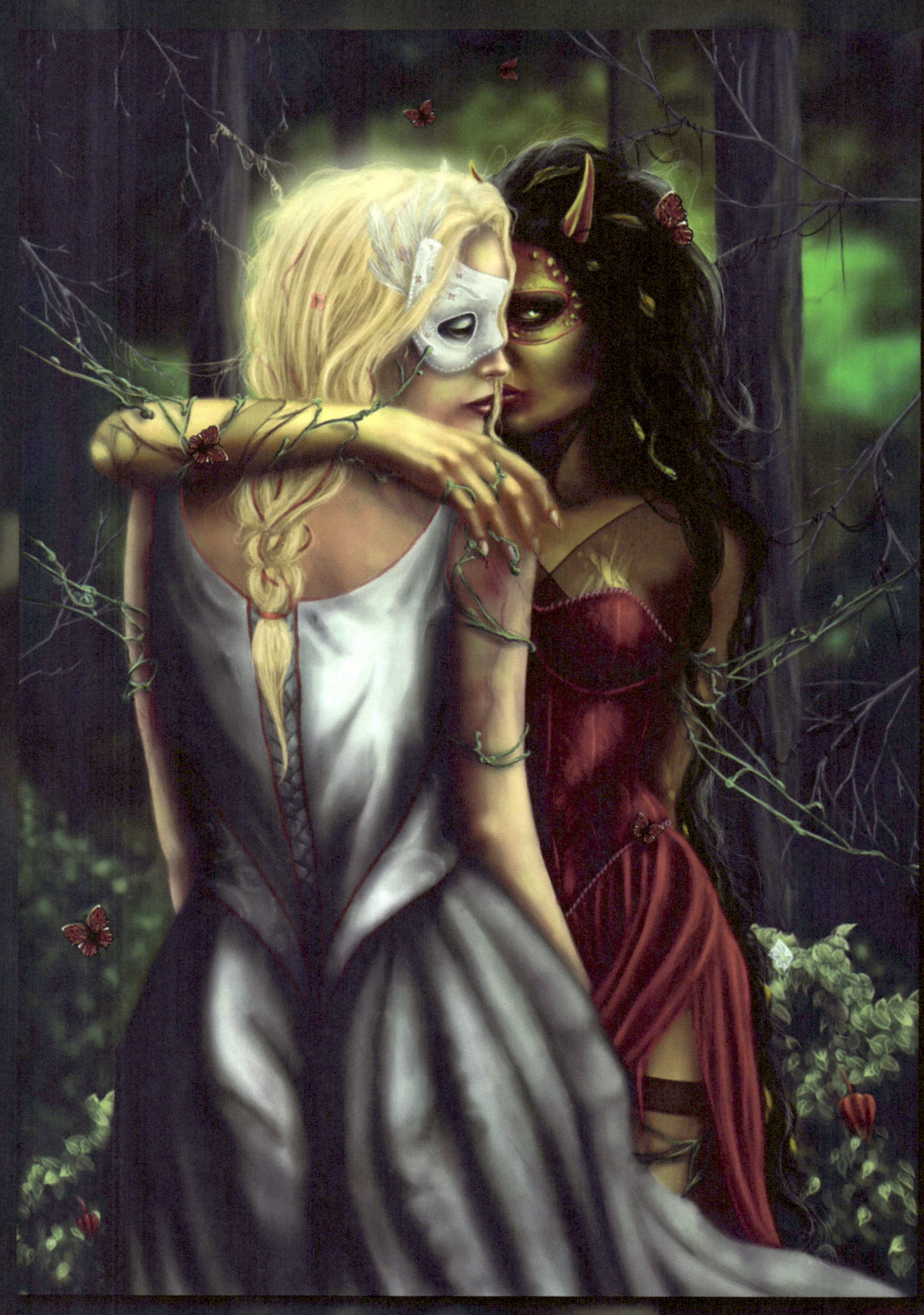

"Possessed", 2008

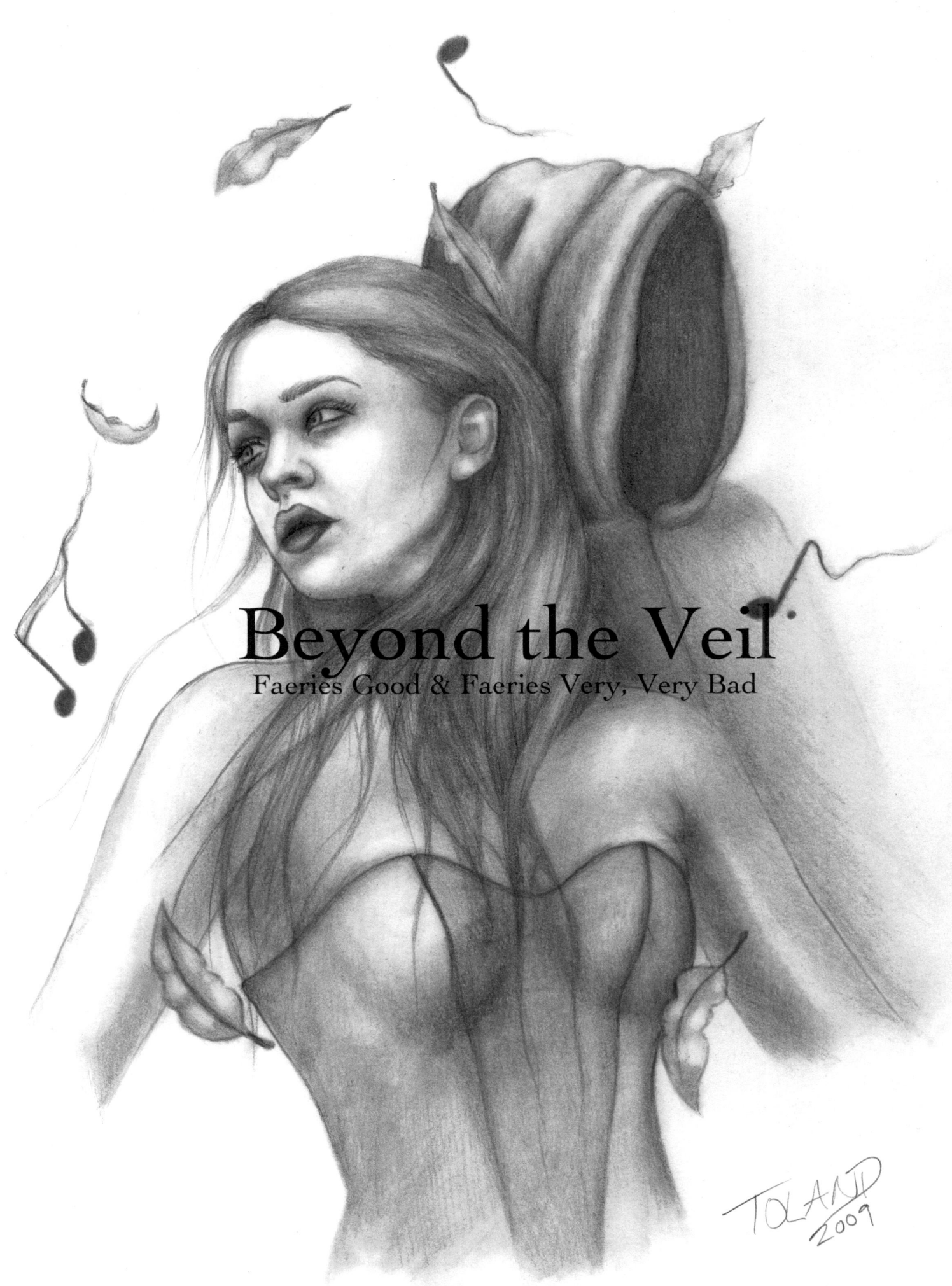

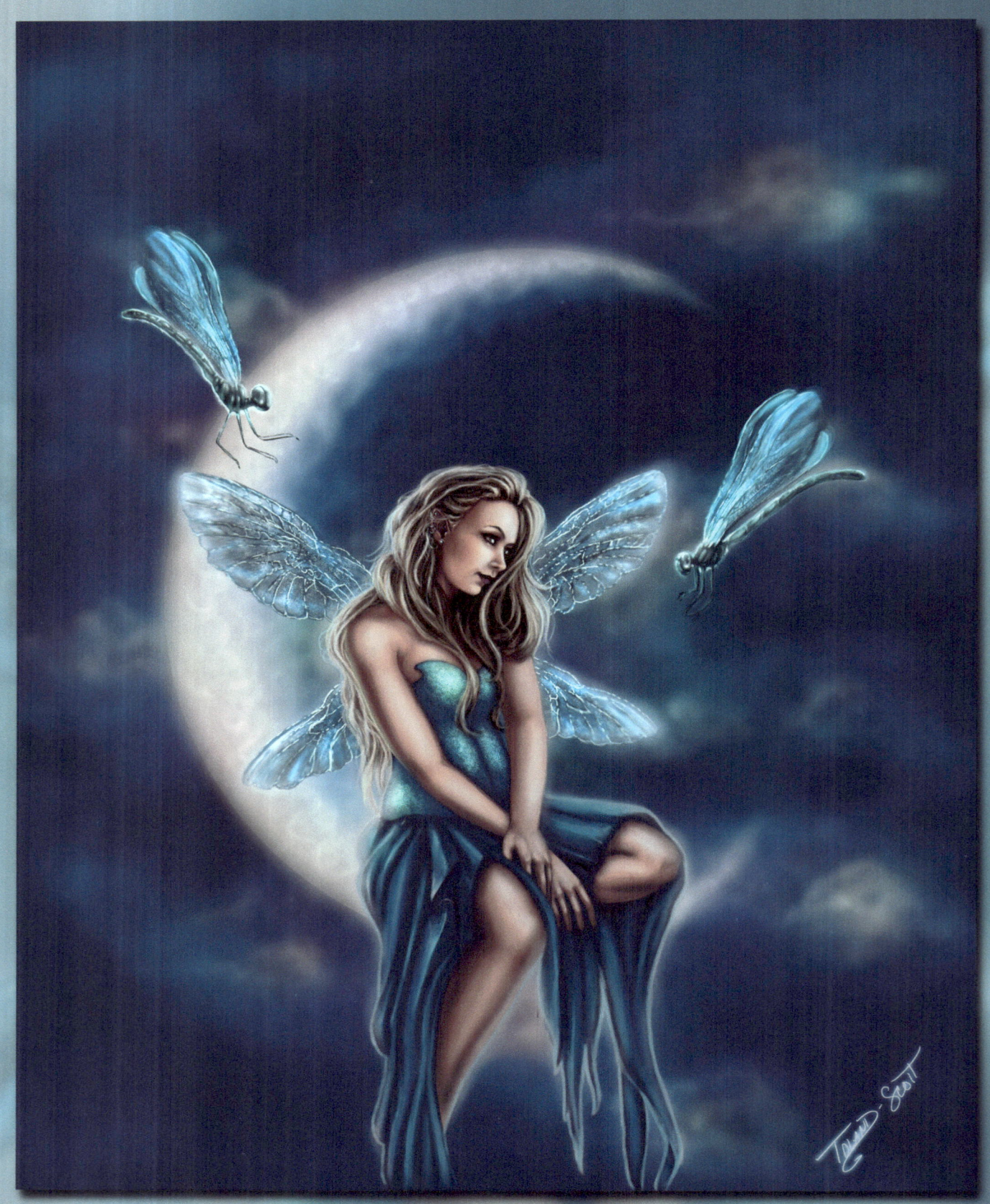

"Dragonfly Moon", 2012

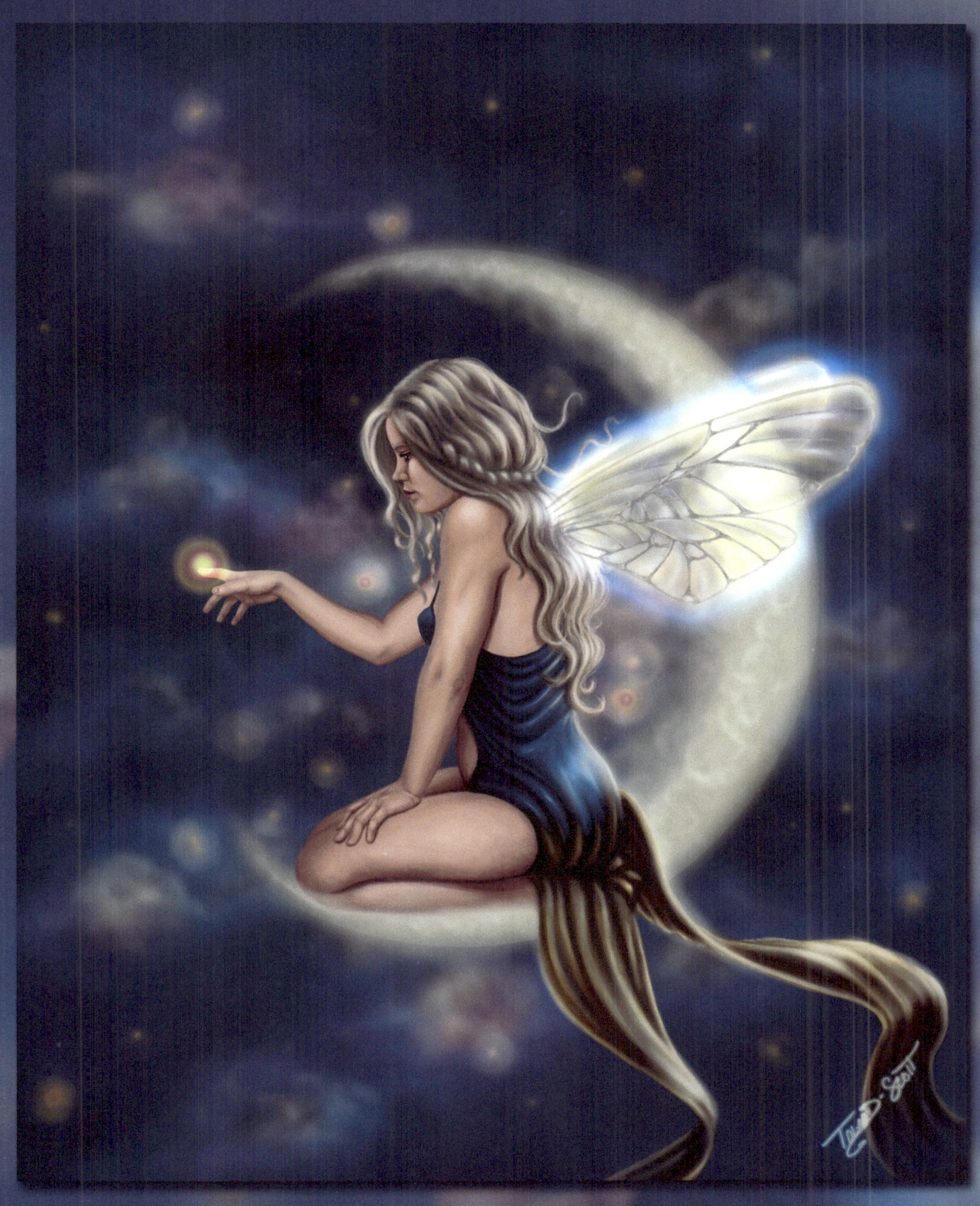

"Firefly Moon", 2012

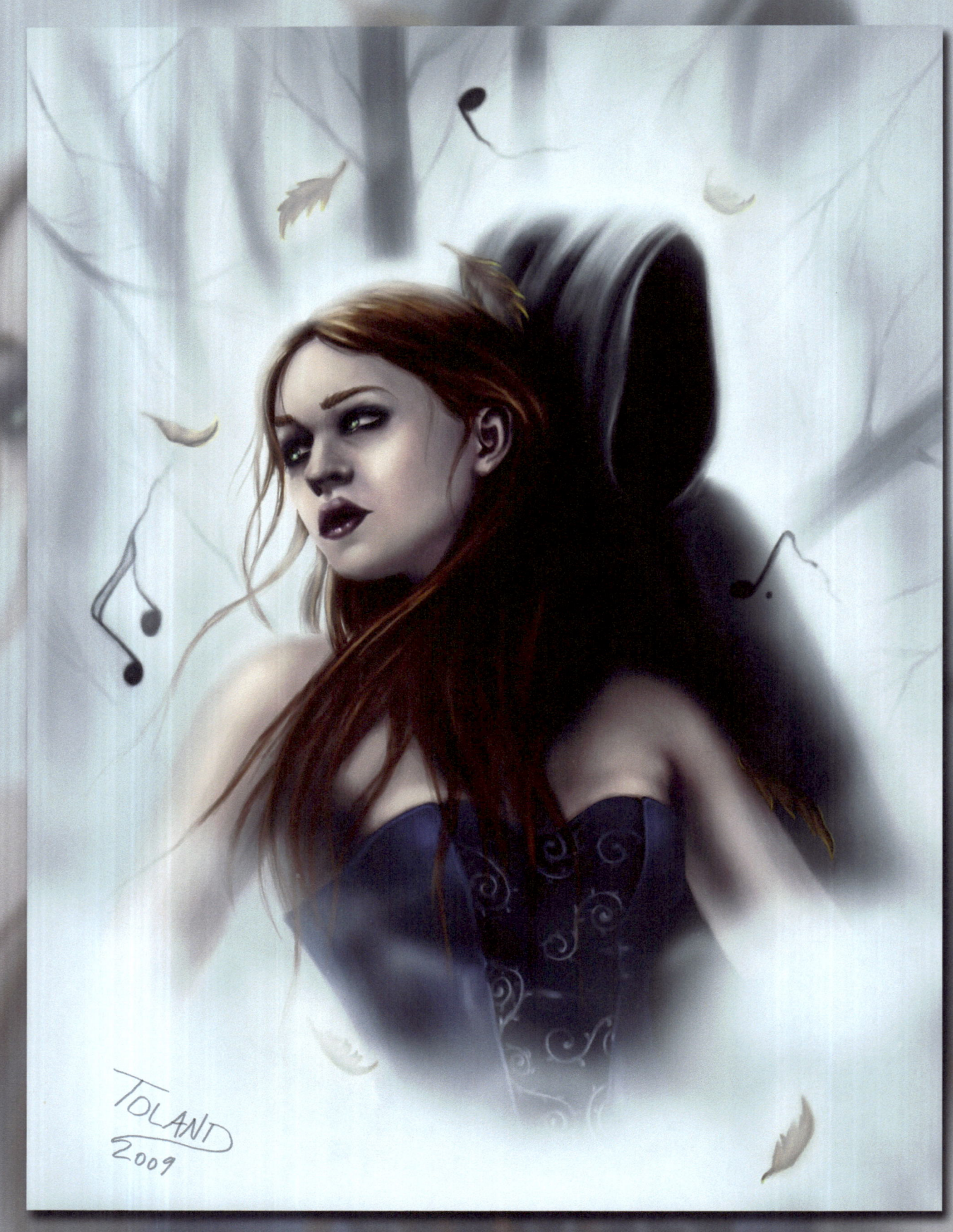

"Haunting Melody", 2009

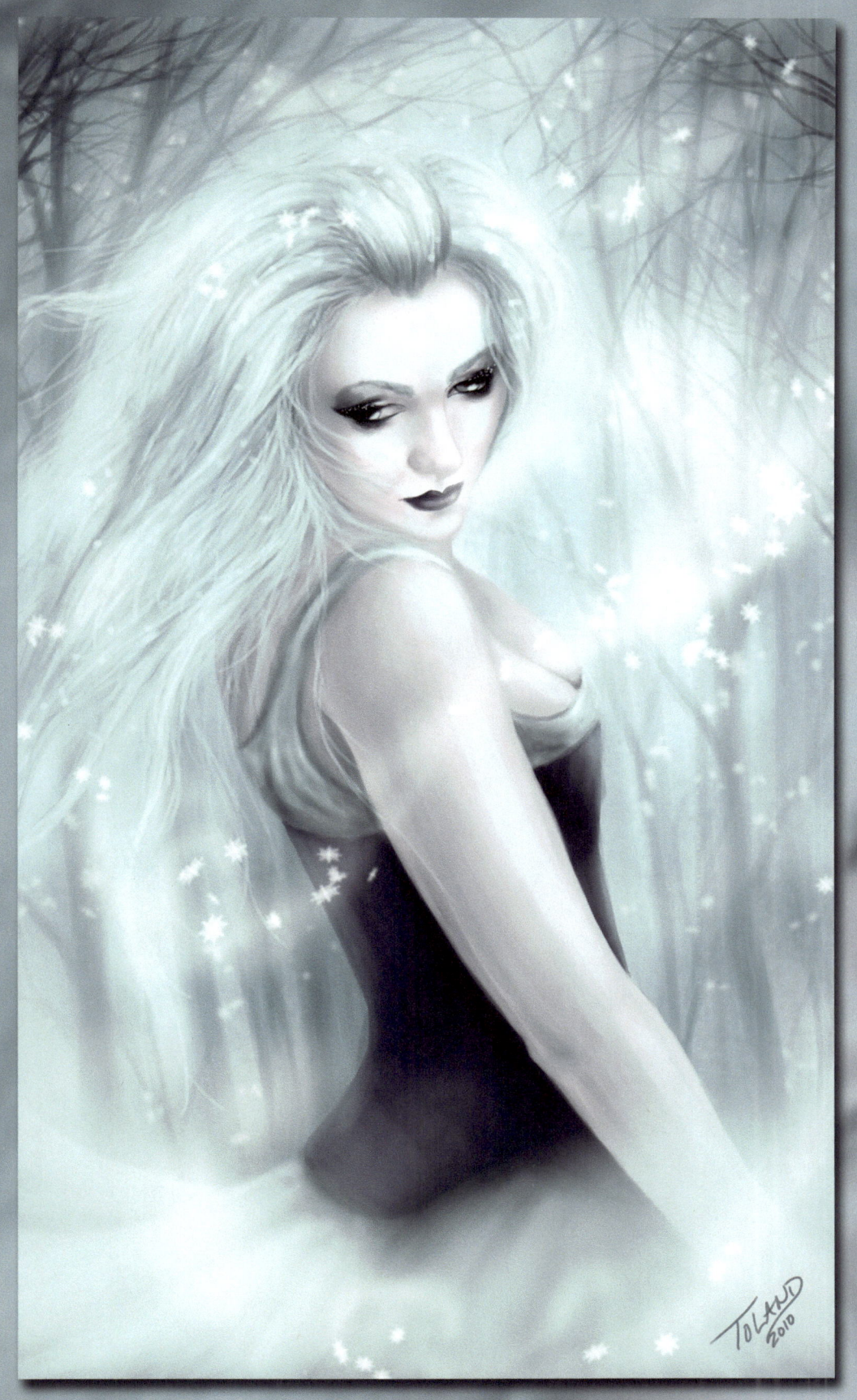

"Winter Soul", 2010

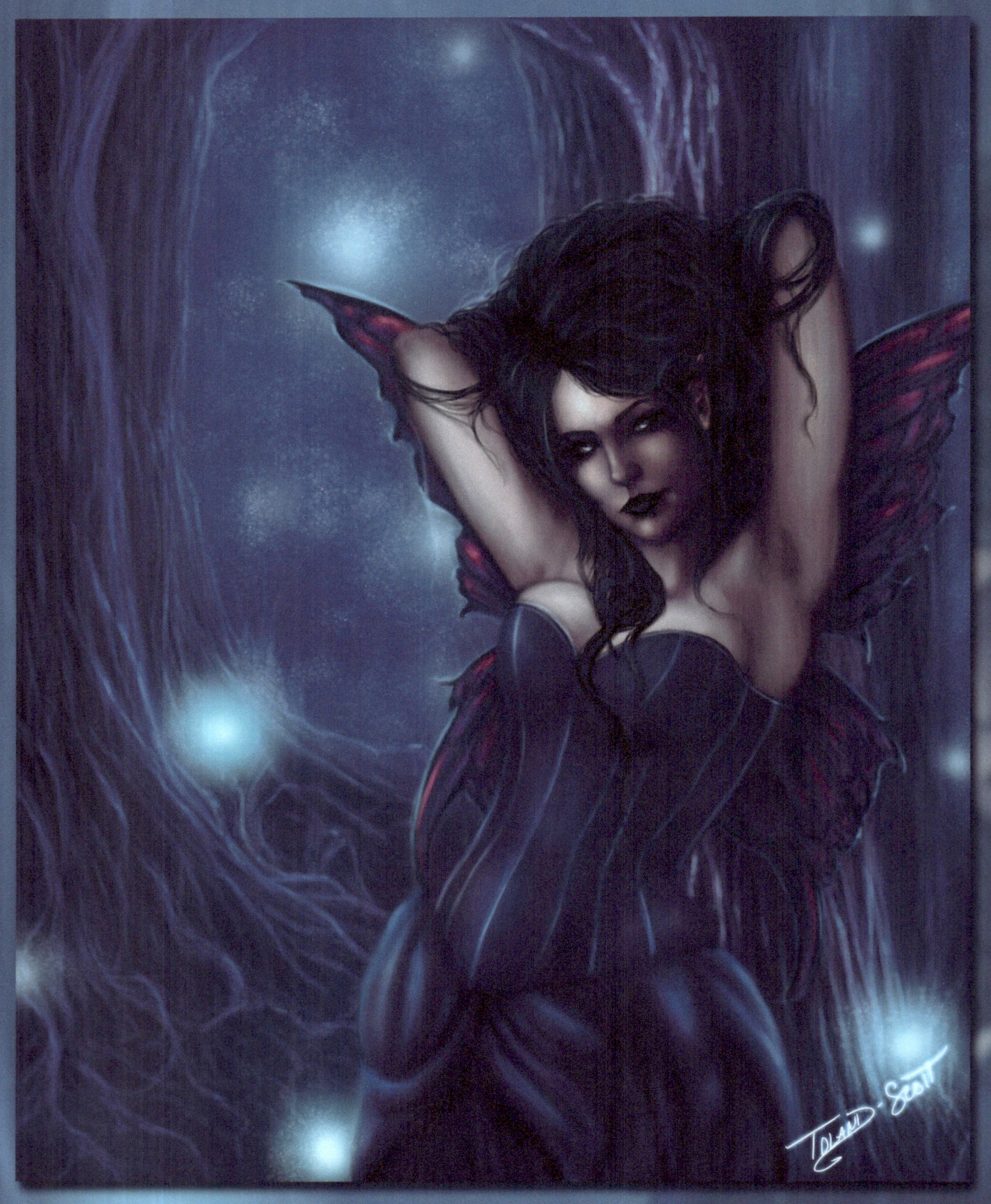

"The Will-o-the-Wisp", 2012

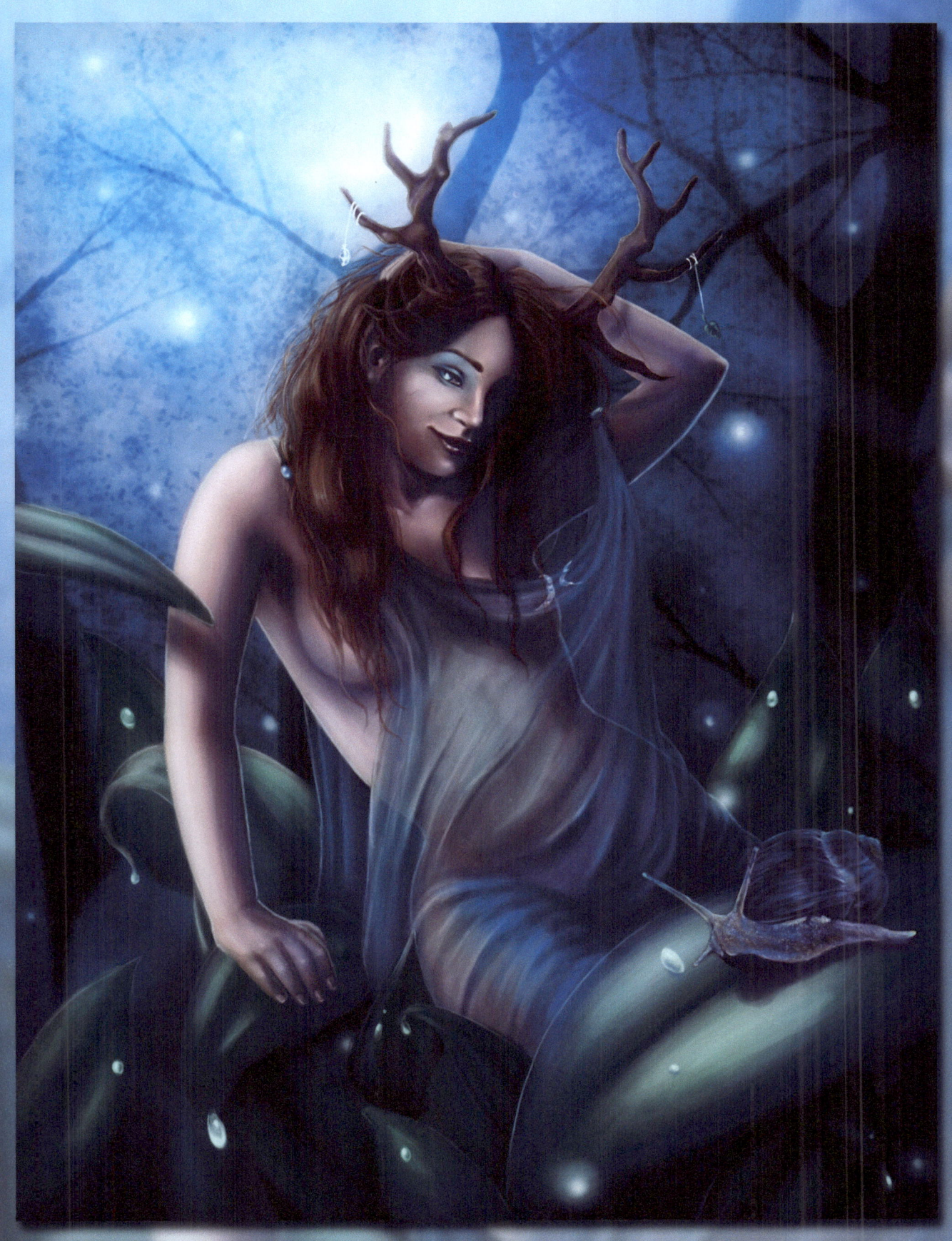

"Queen of the Wood", 2009

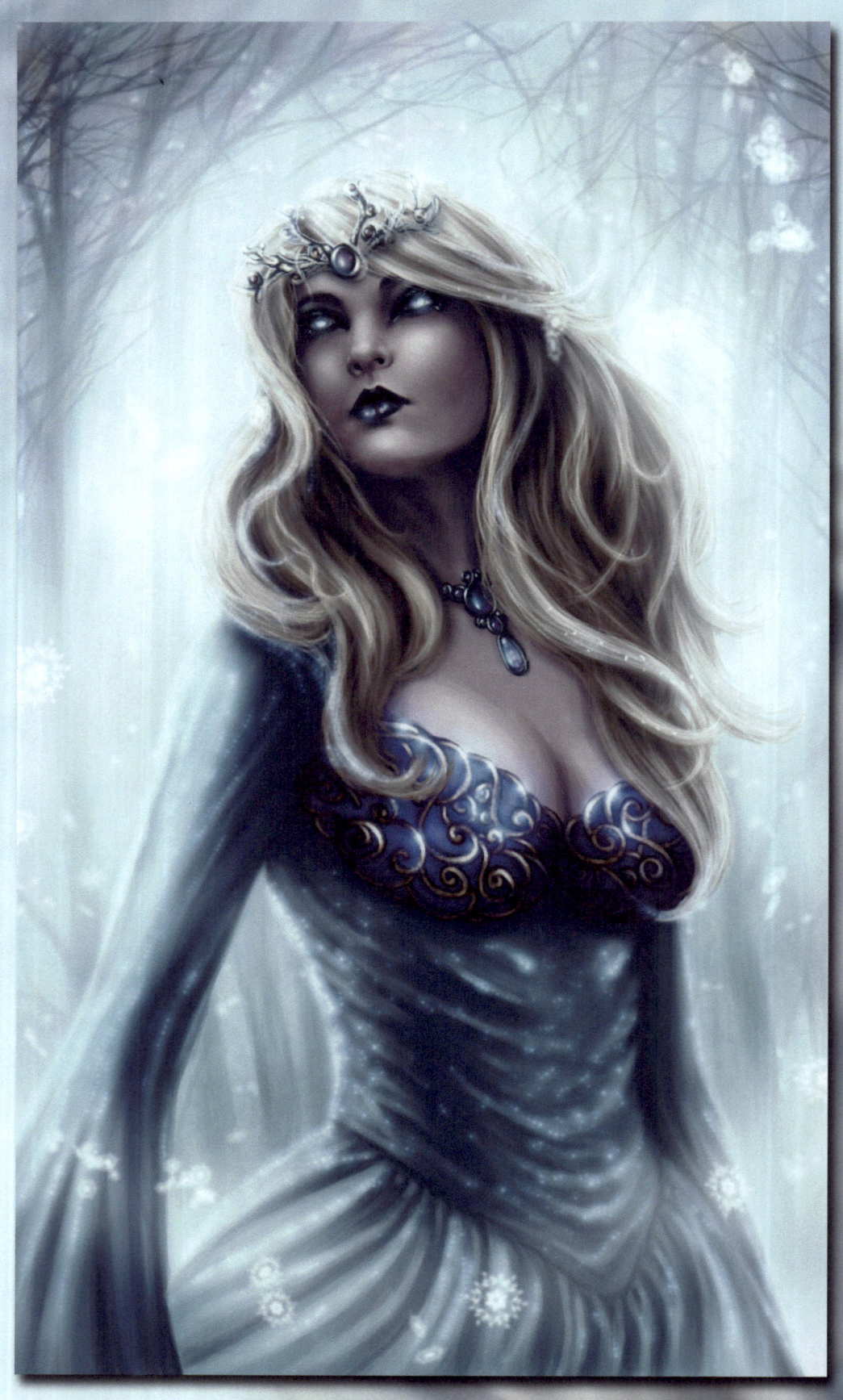

"Winter Queen", 2012

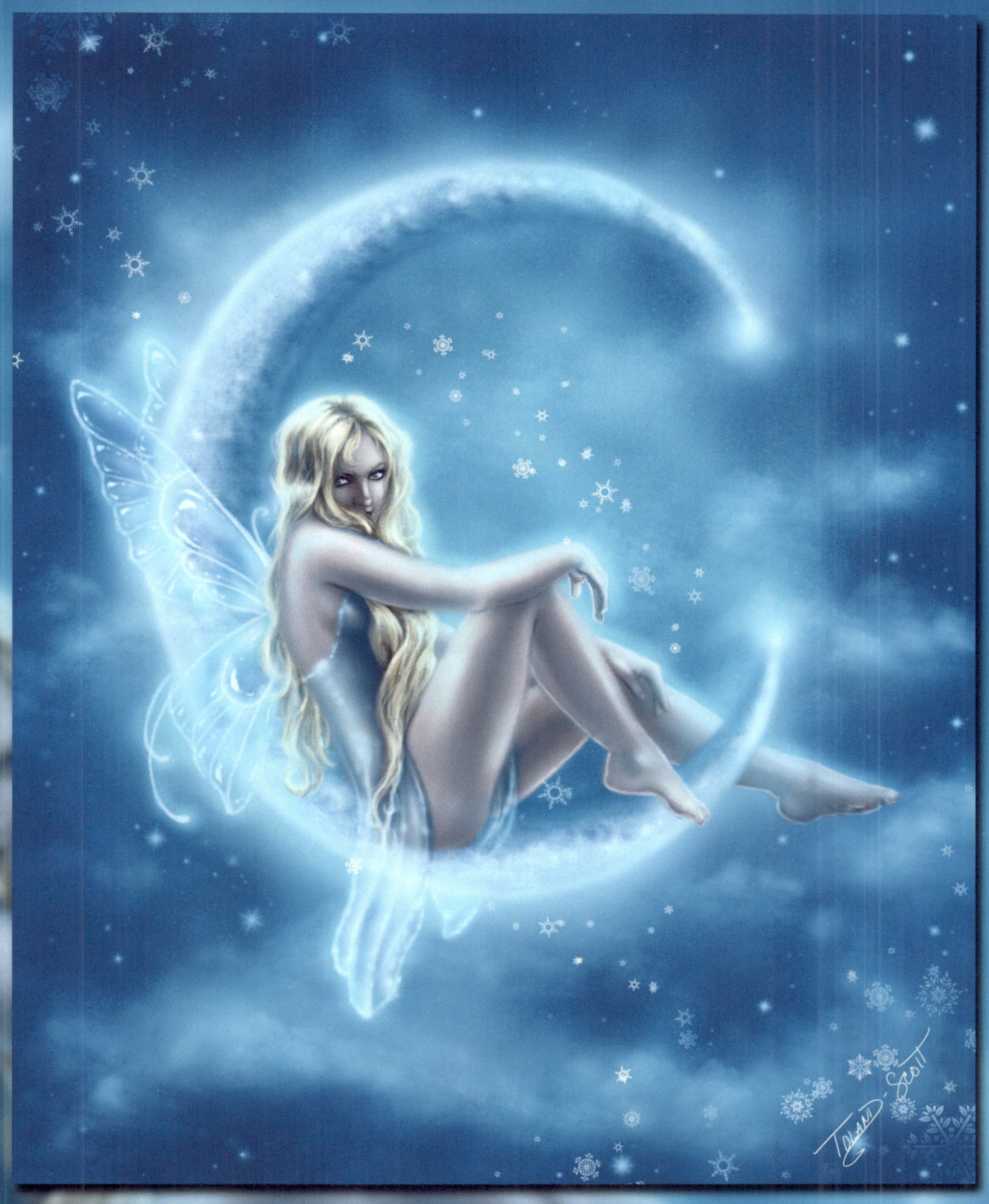

"Winter Moon", 2011

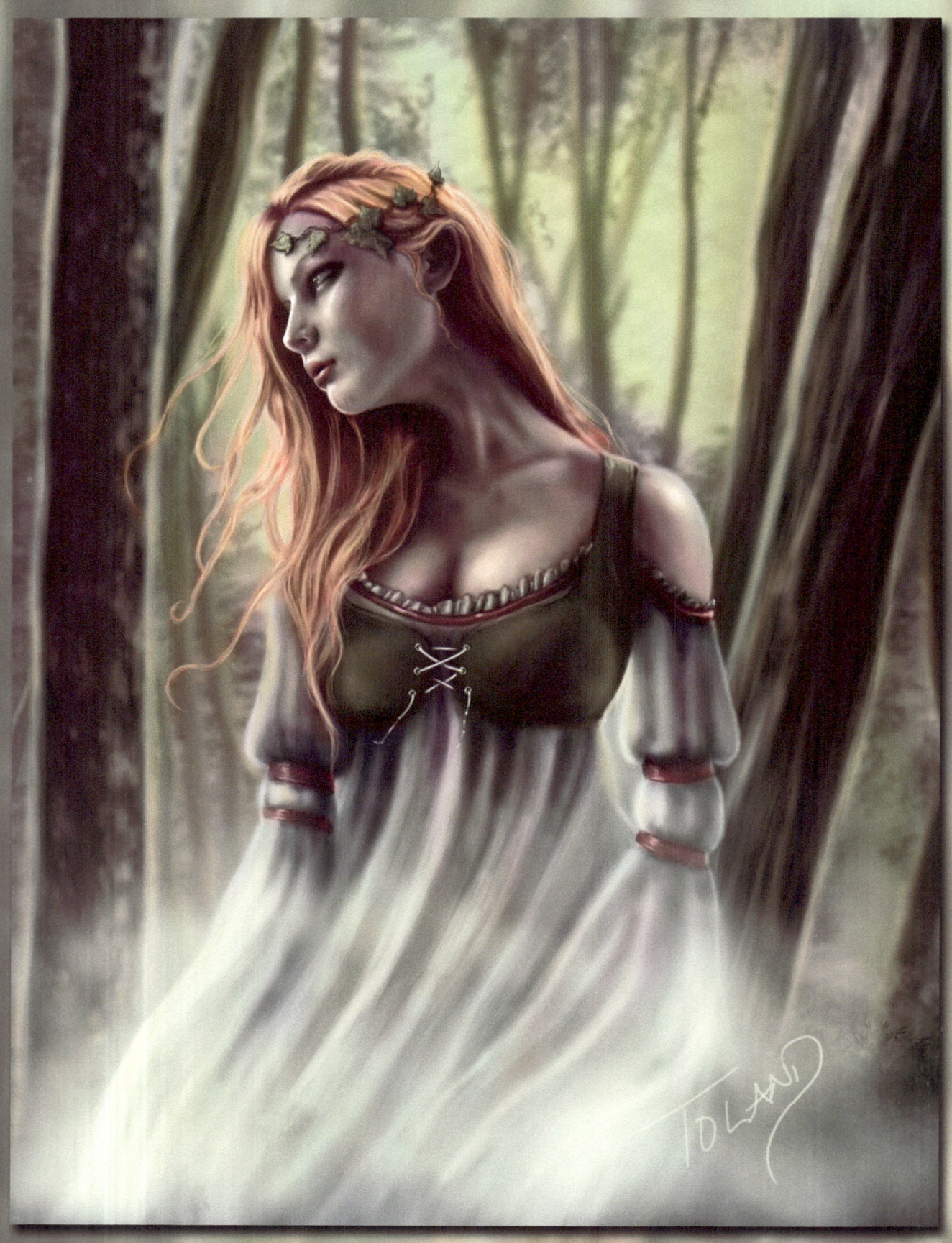

"Beneath the Ivy", 2010

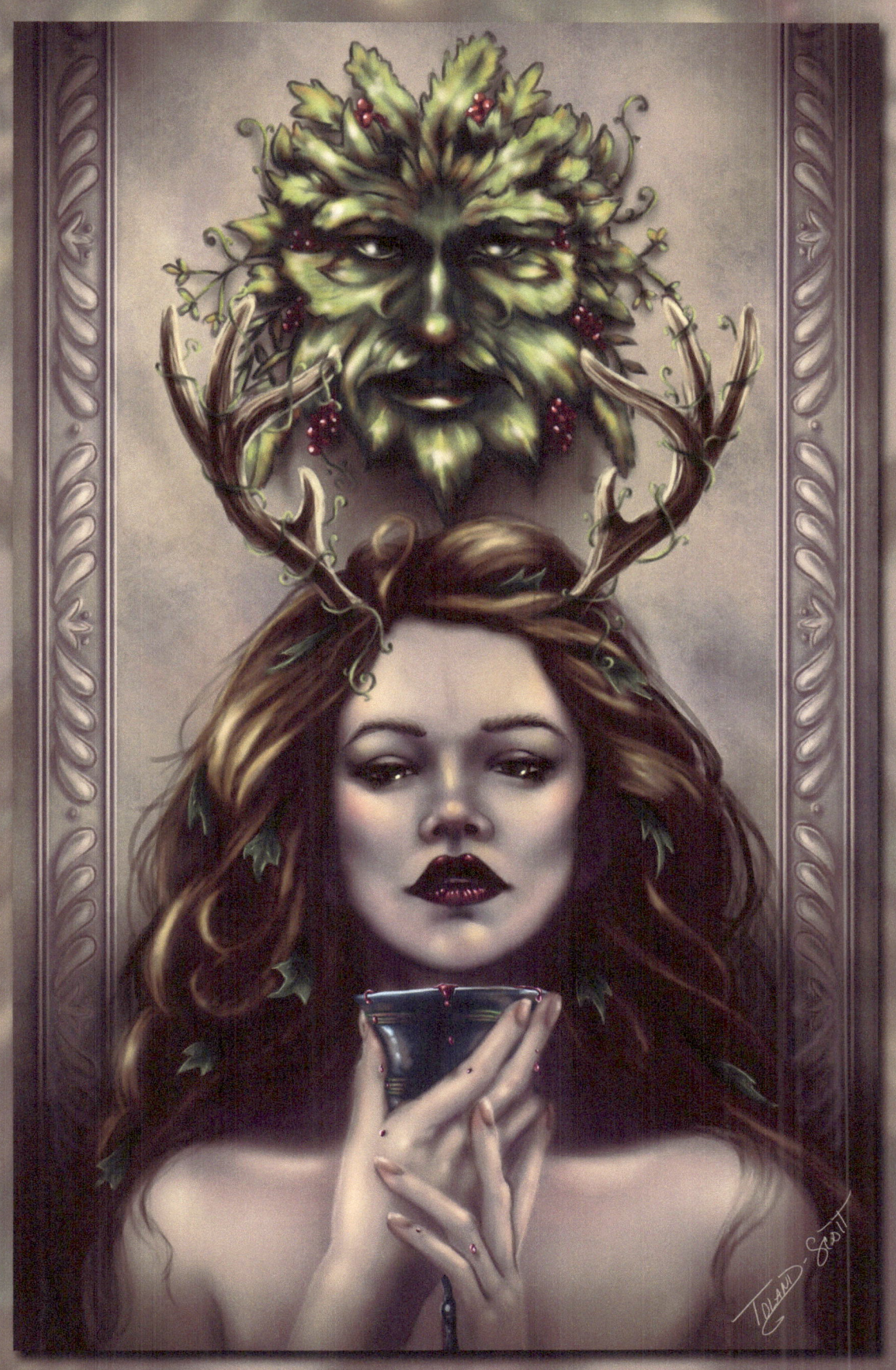

"Abundance", 2011

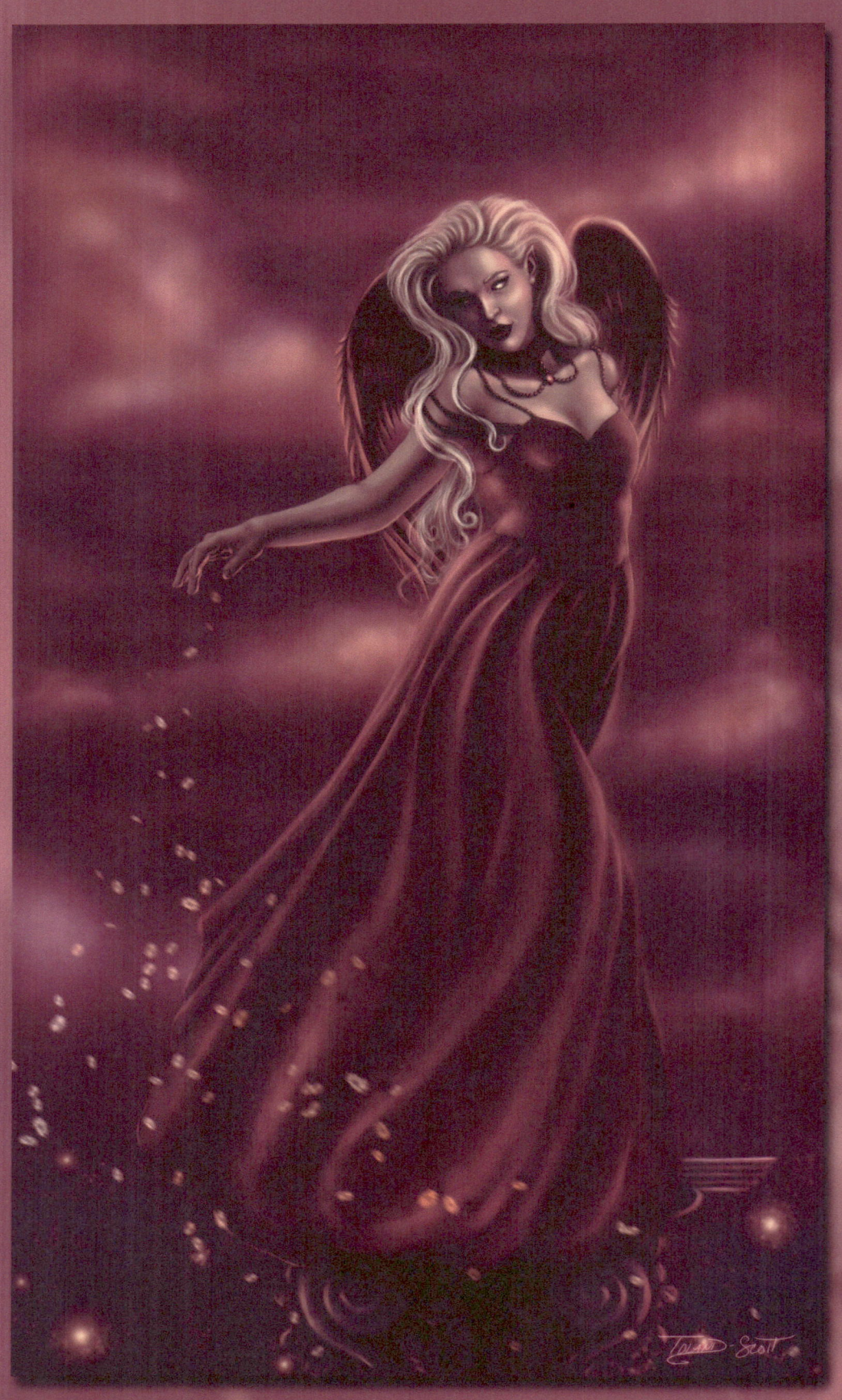

"Princess of Hearts", 2012

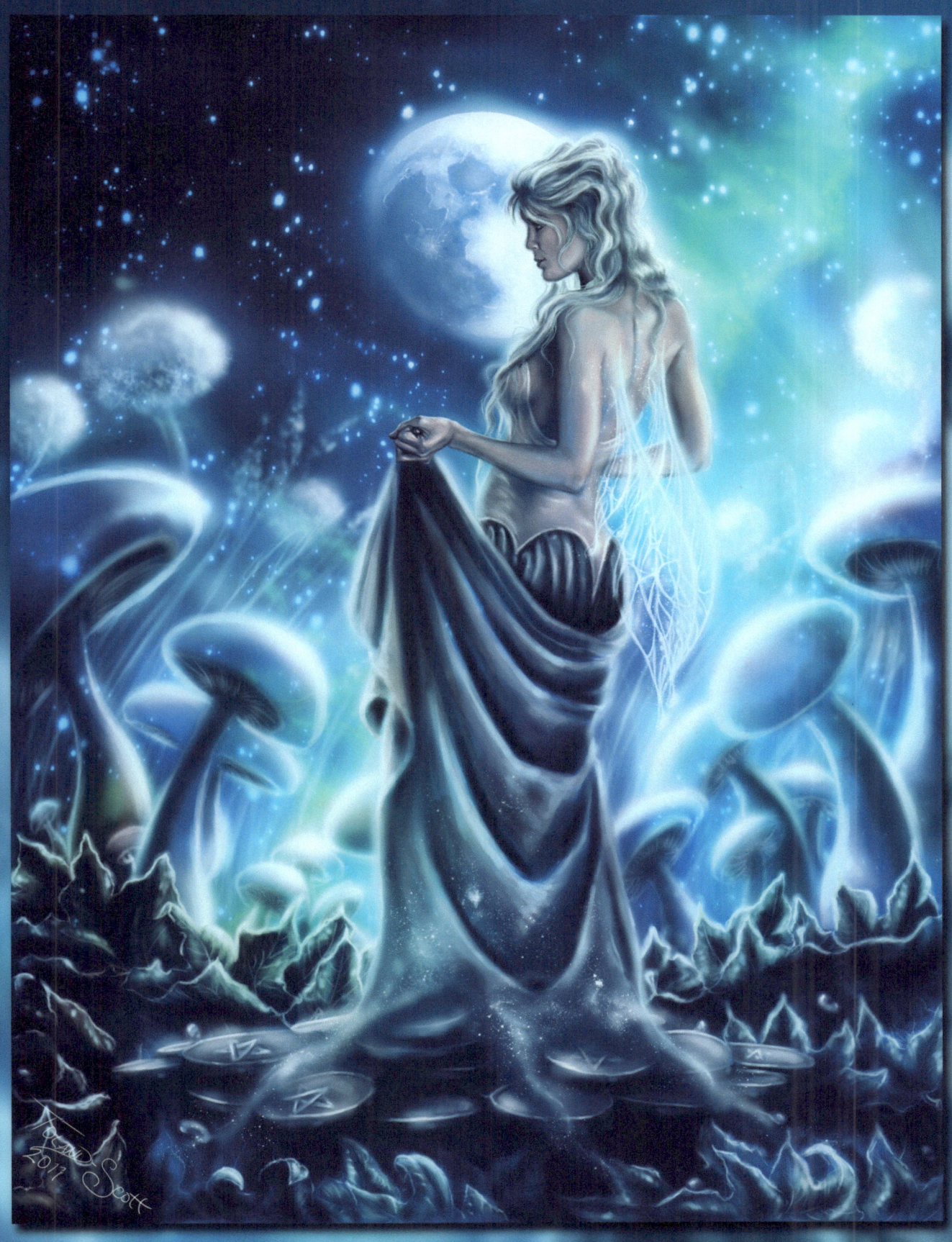

"Tricky Treasures", 2011

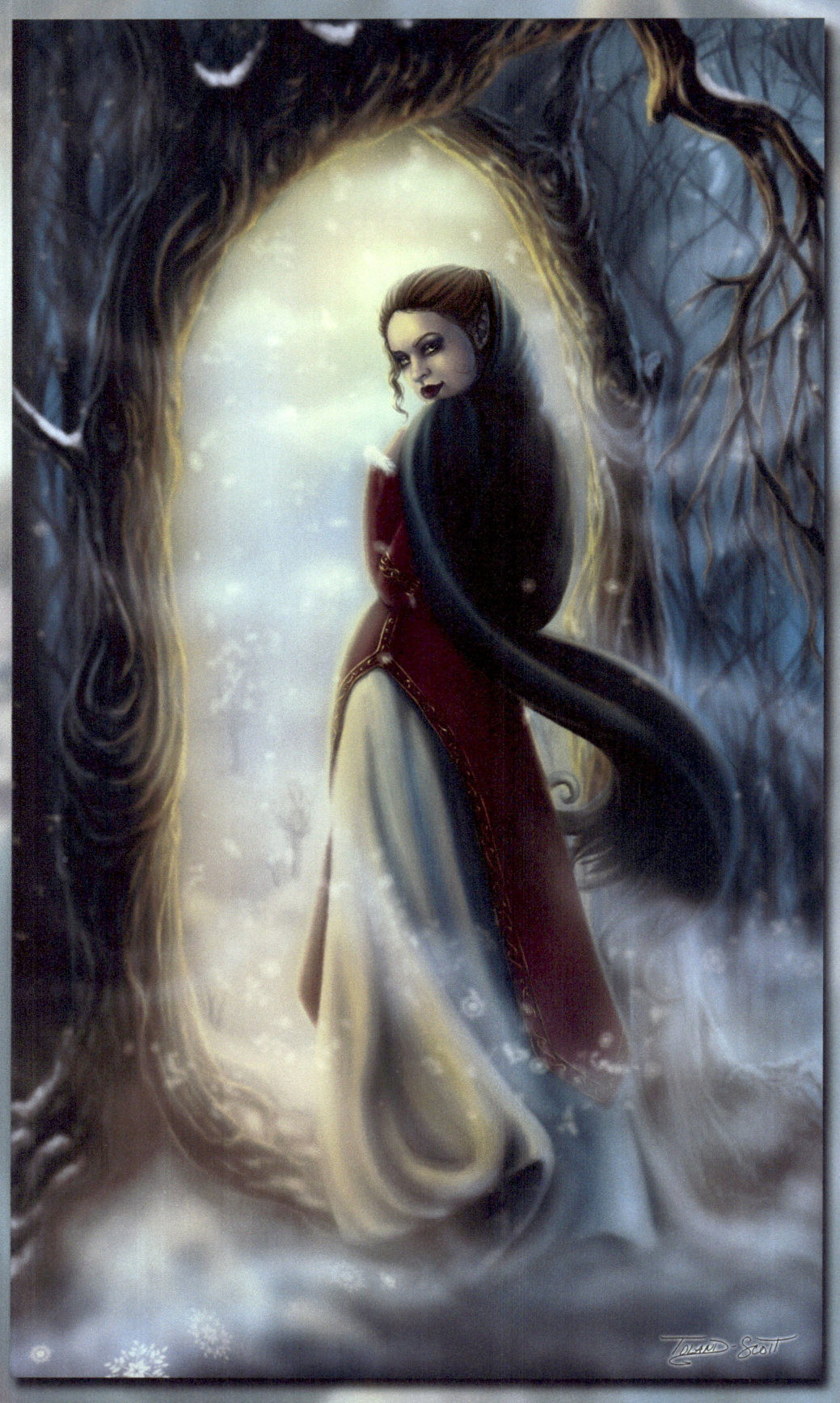

"Winter's Passage", 2012

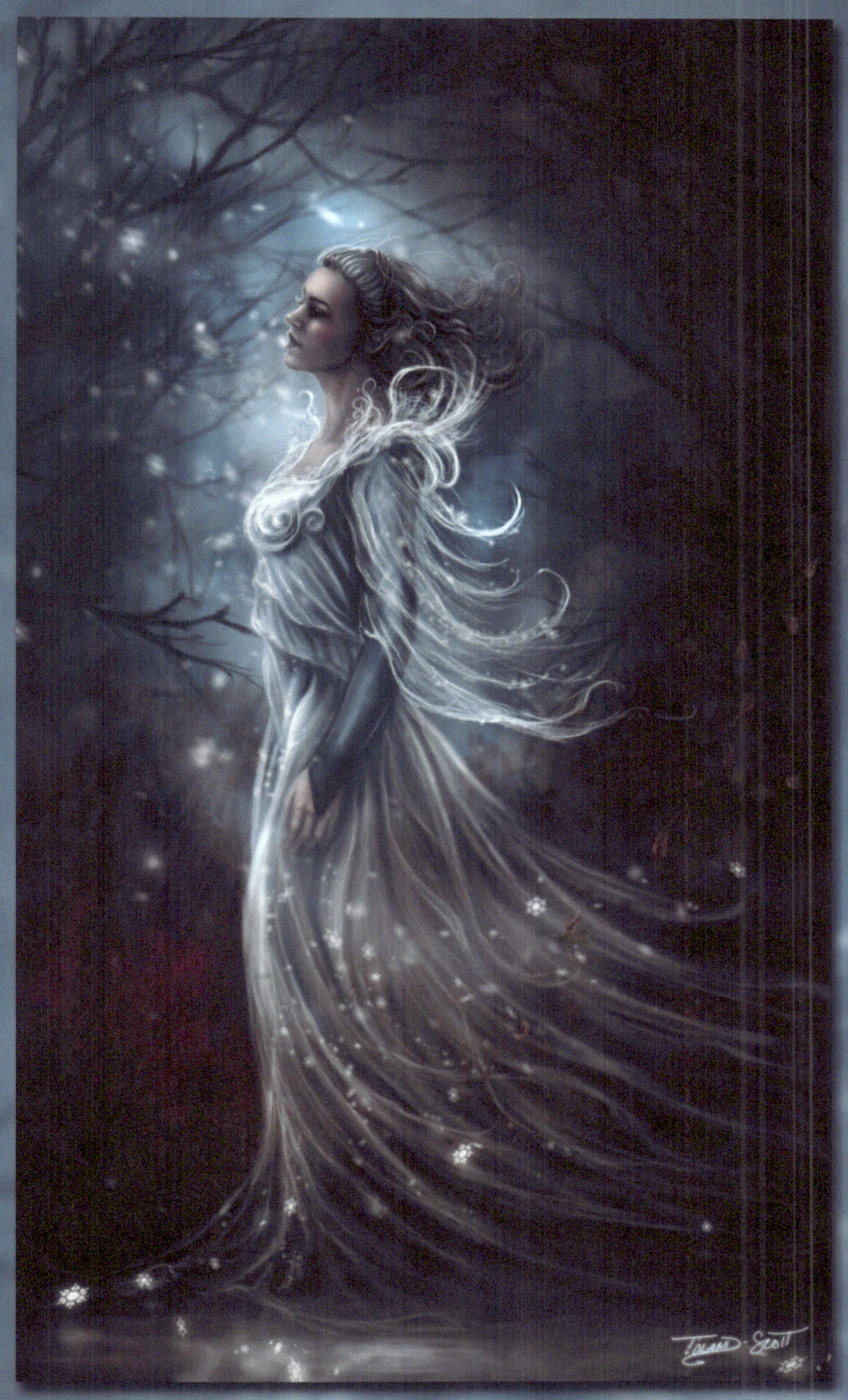

"First Kiss of Frost", 2012

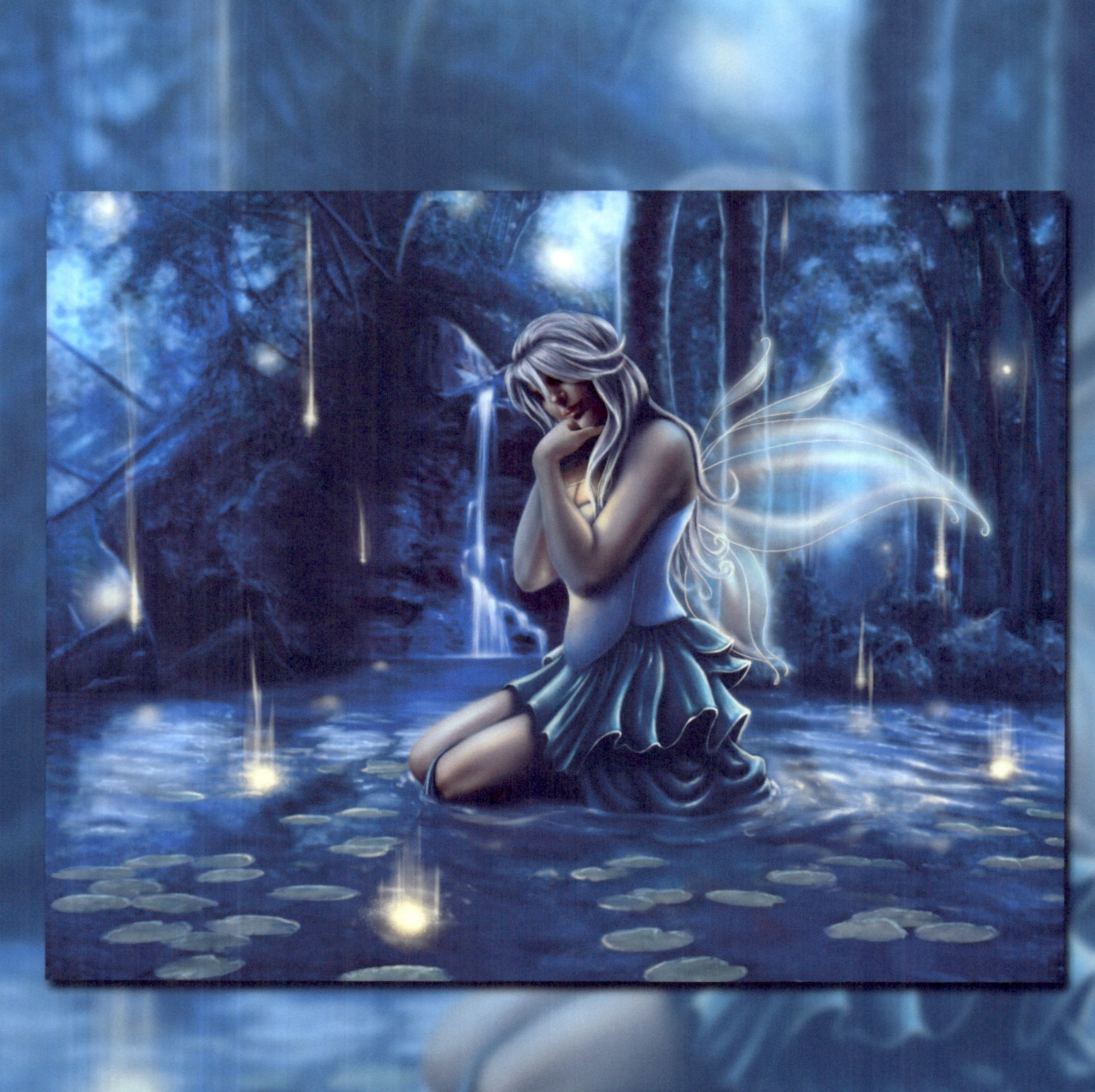

"Stardust", 2011

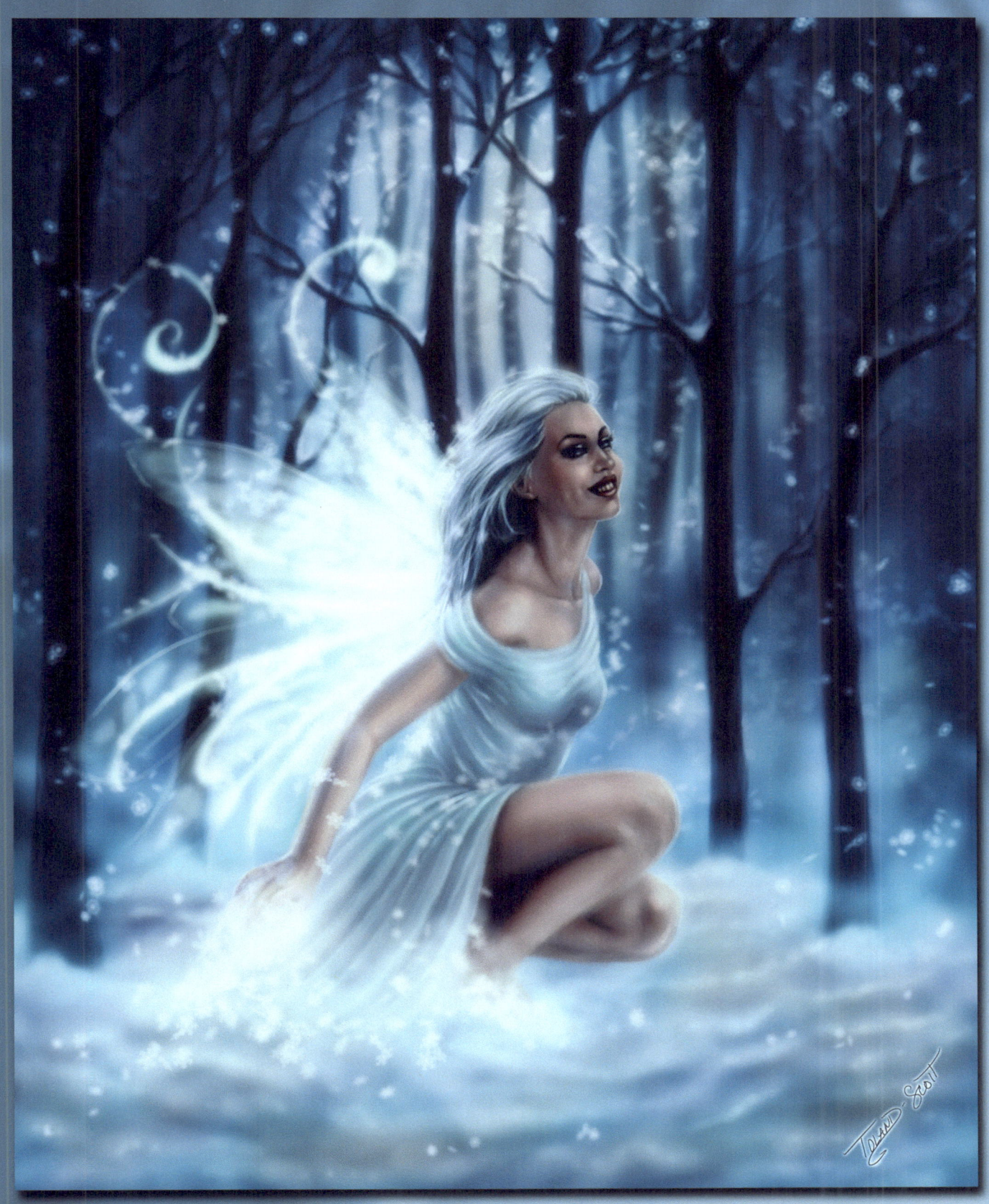

"Awaking Winter", 2012

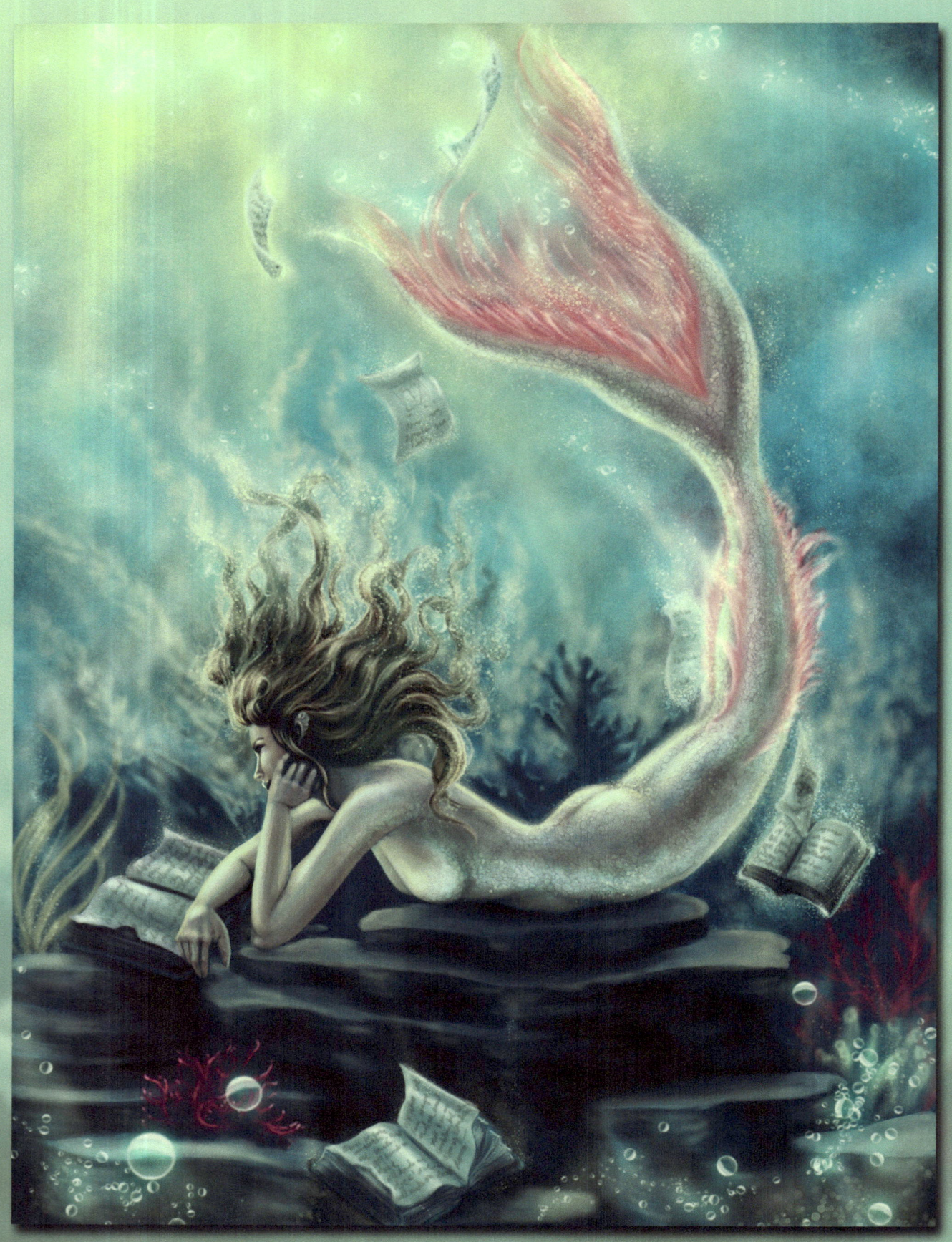

"Lost Books", 2012

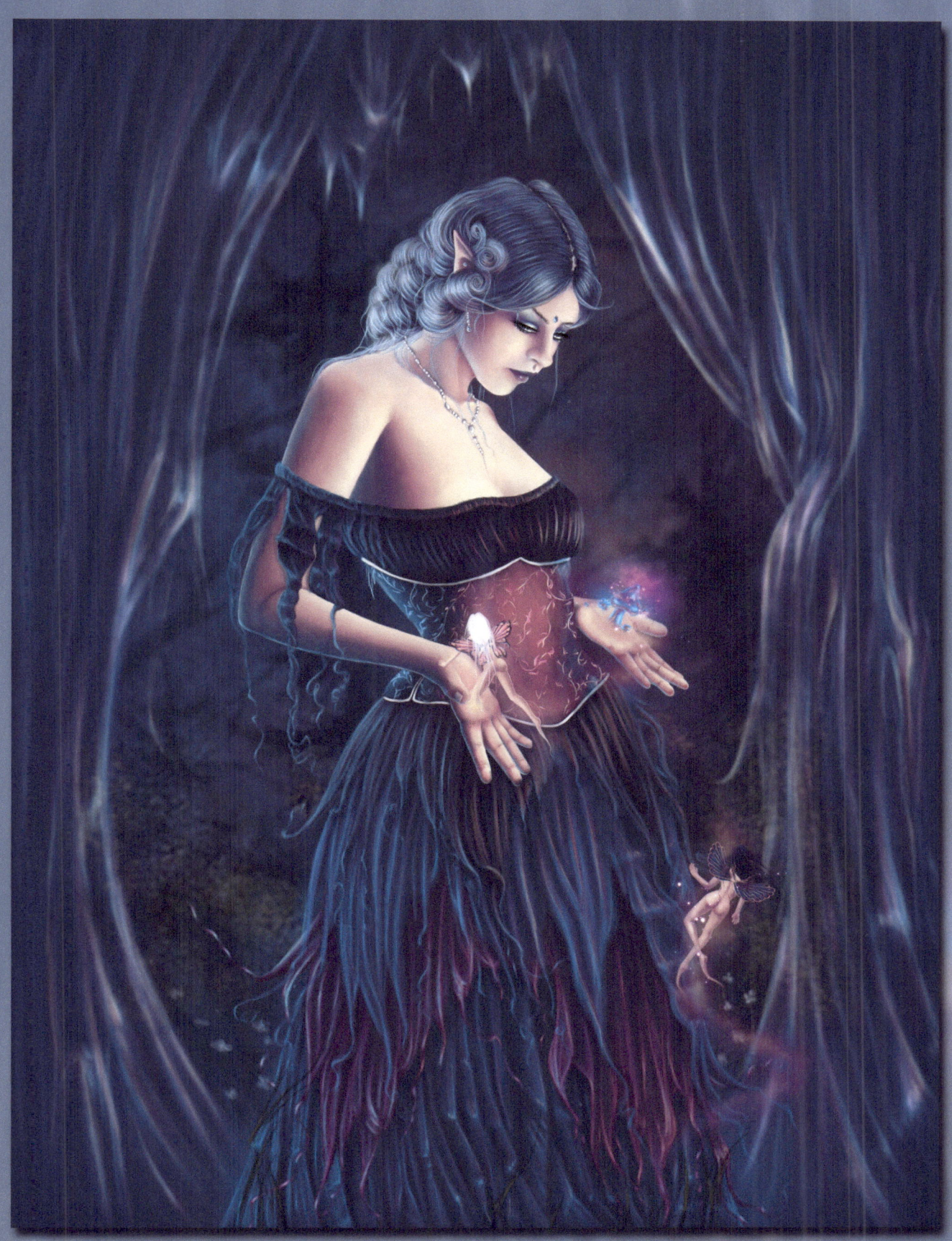

"Birth", 2008

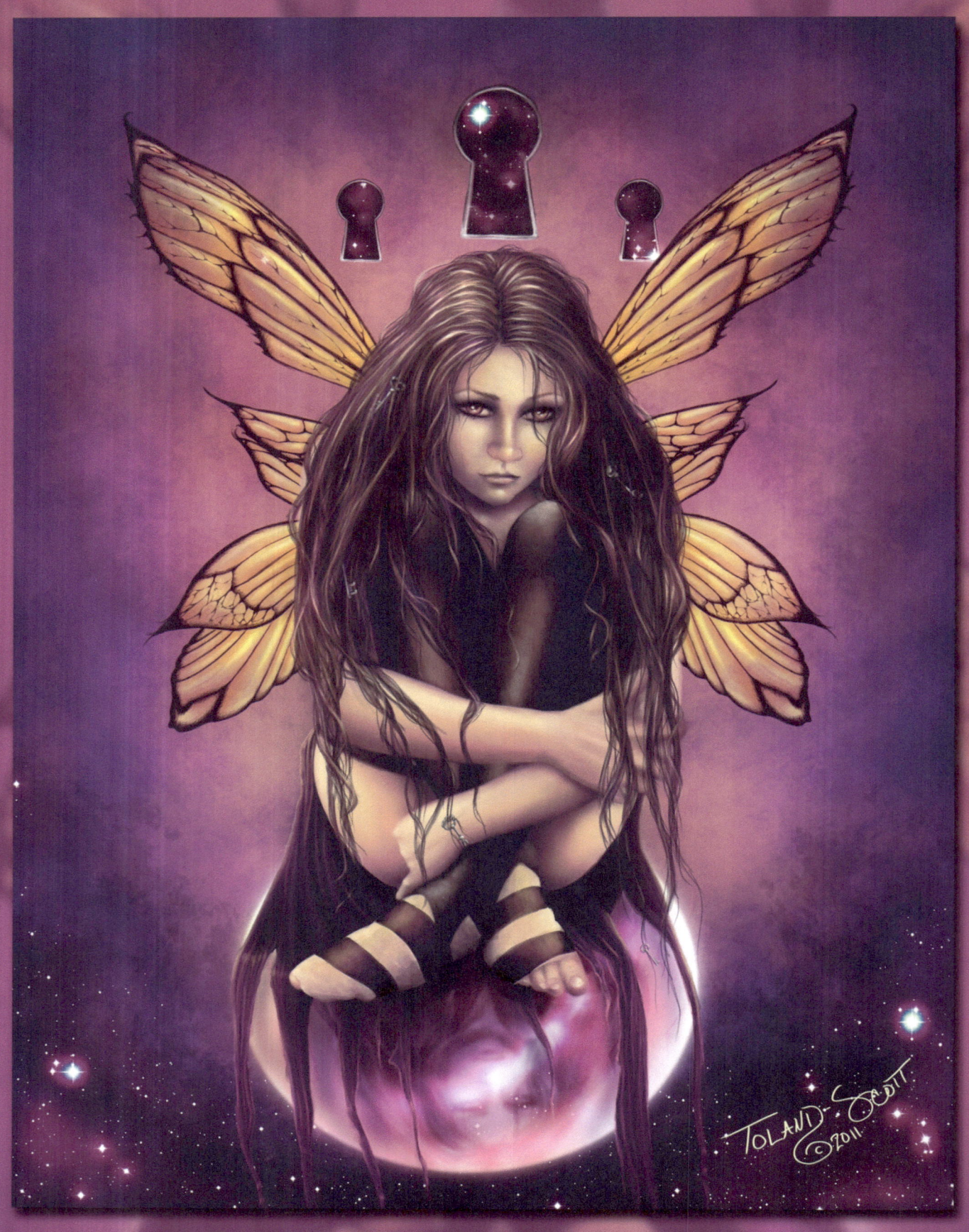

"Keeper of Secrets", 2008 (re-released in 2011)

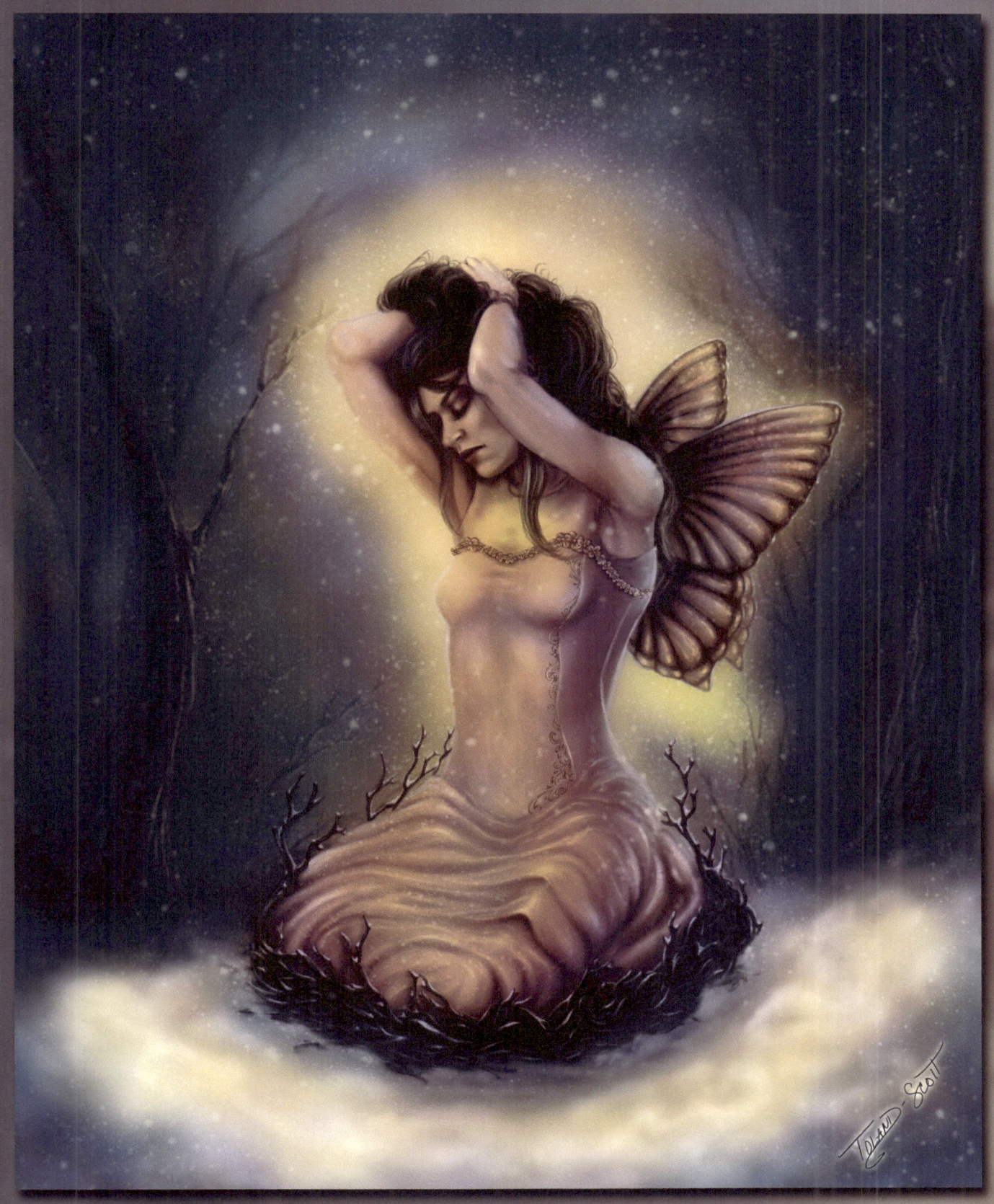

"Winterborn", 2012

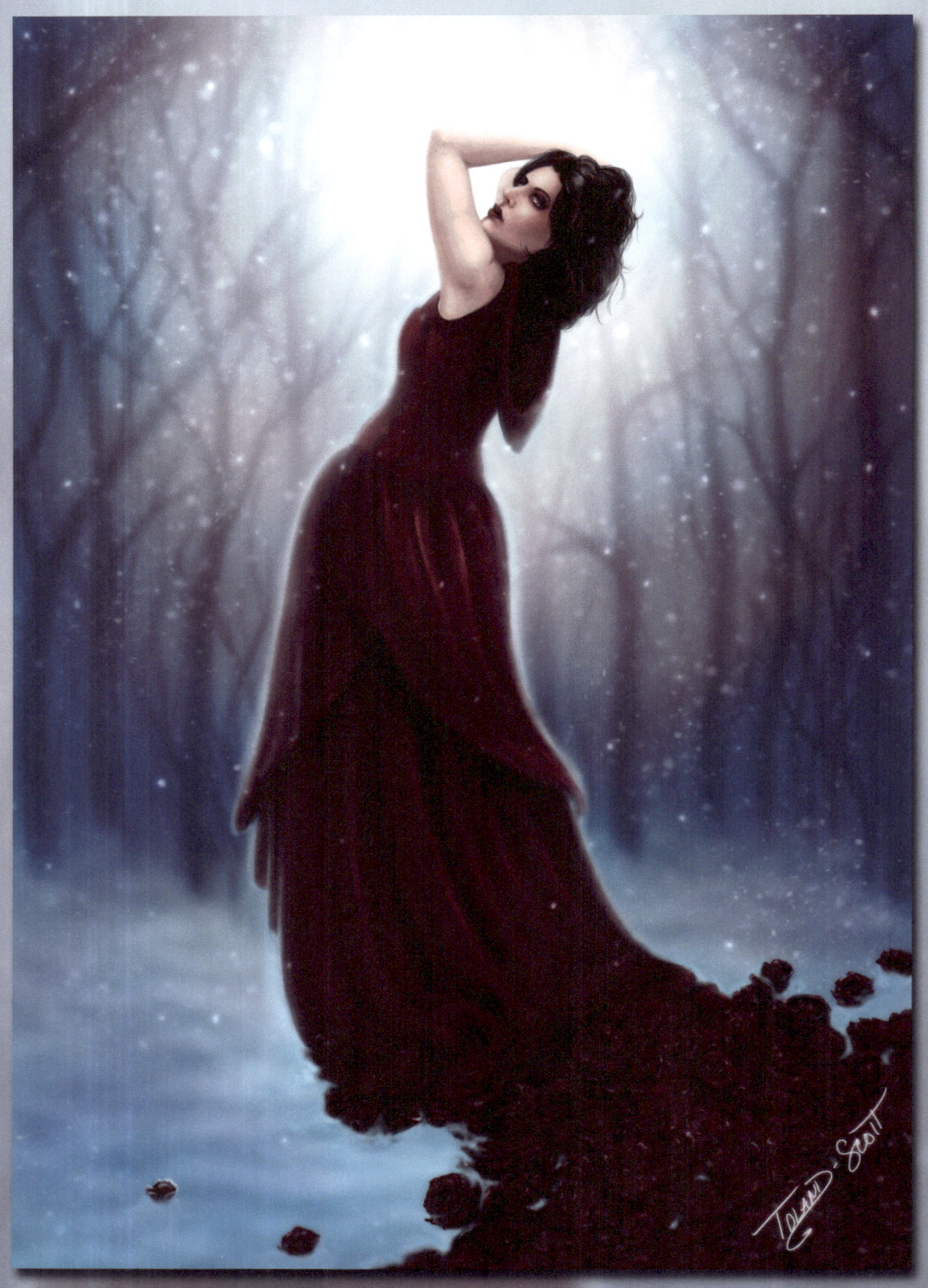

"Last Rose of Summer", 2012

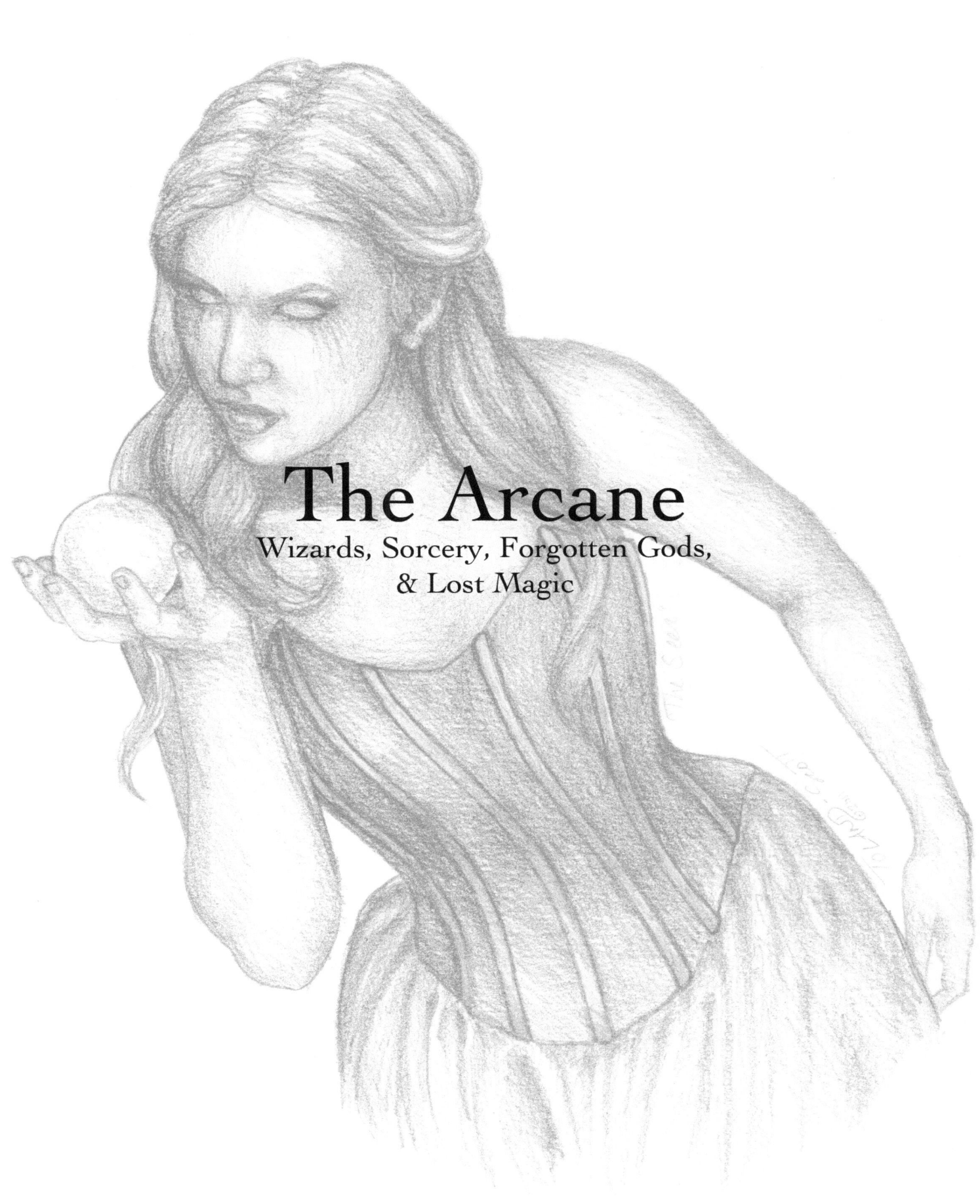

The Arcane
Wizards, Sorcery, Forgotten Gods,
& Lost Magic

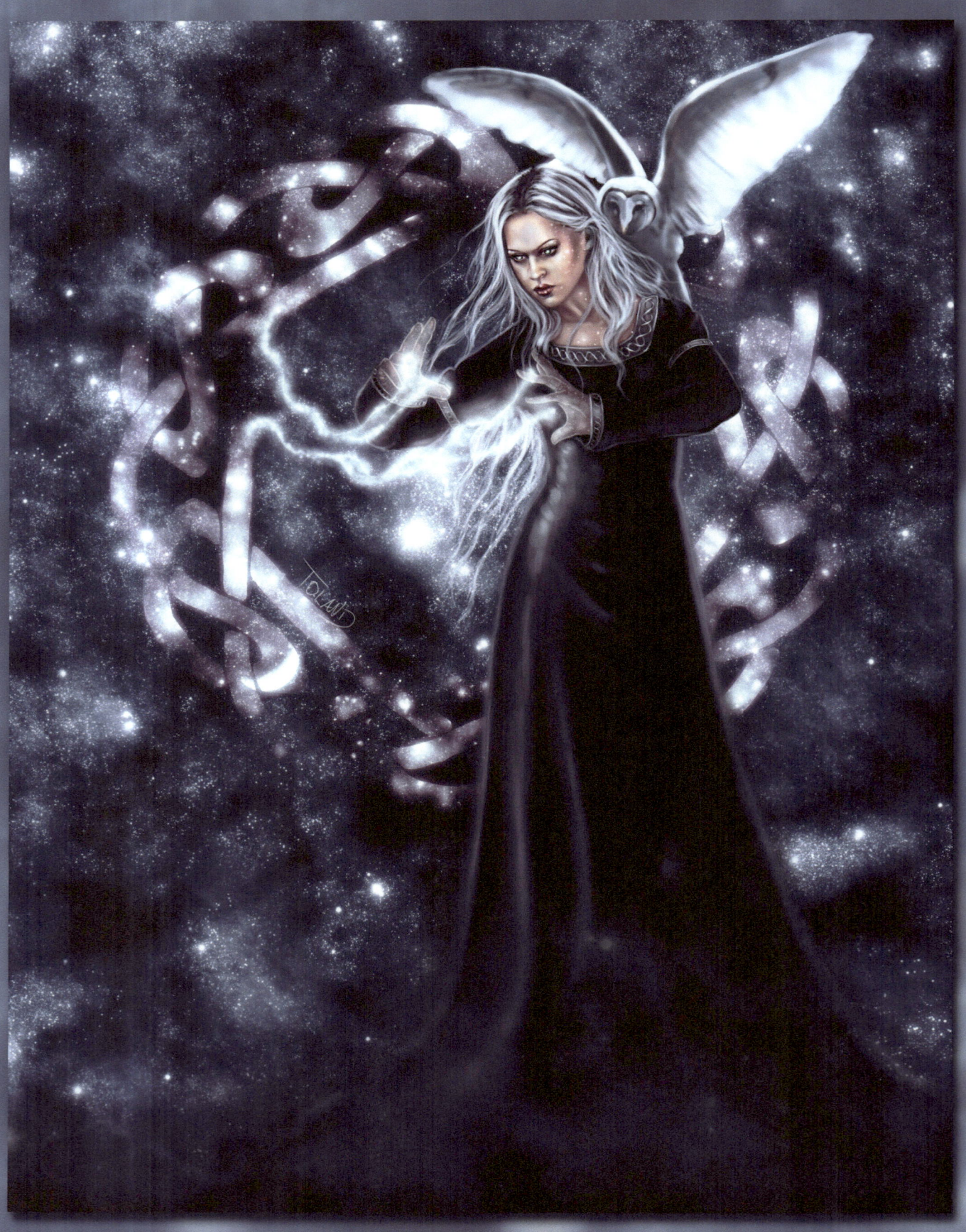

"Arianrhod", 2010

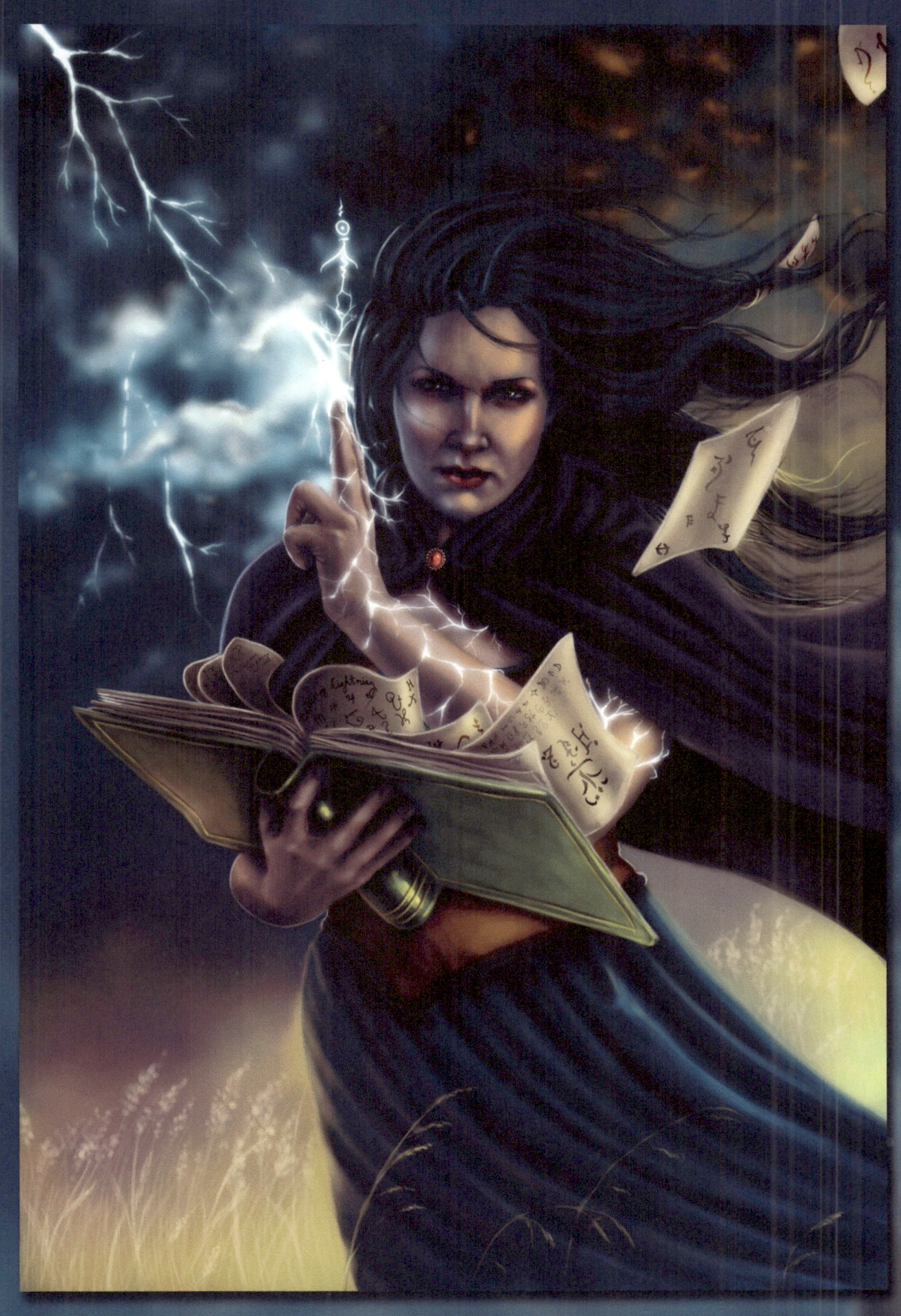

"Calling the Storm", 2010

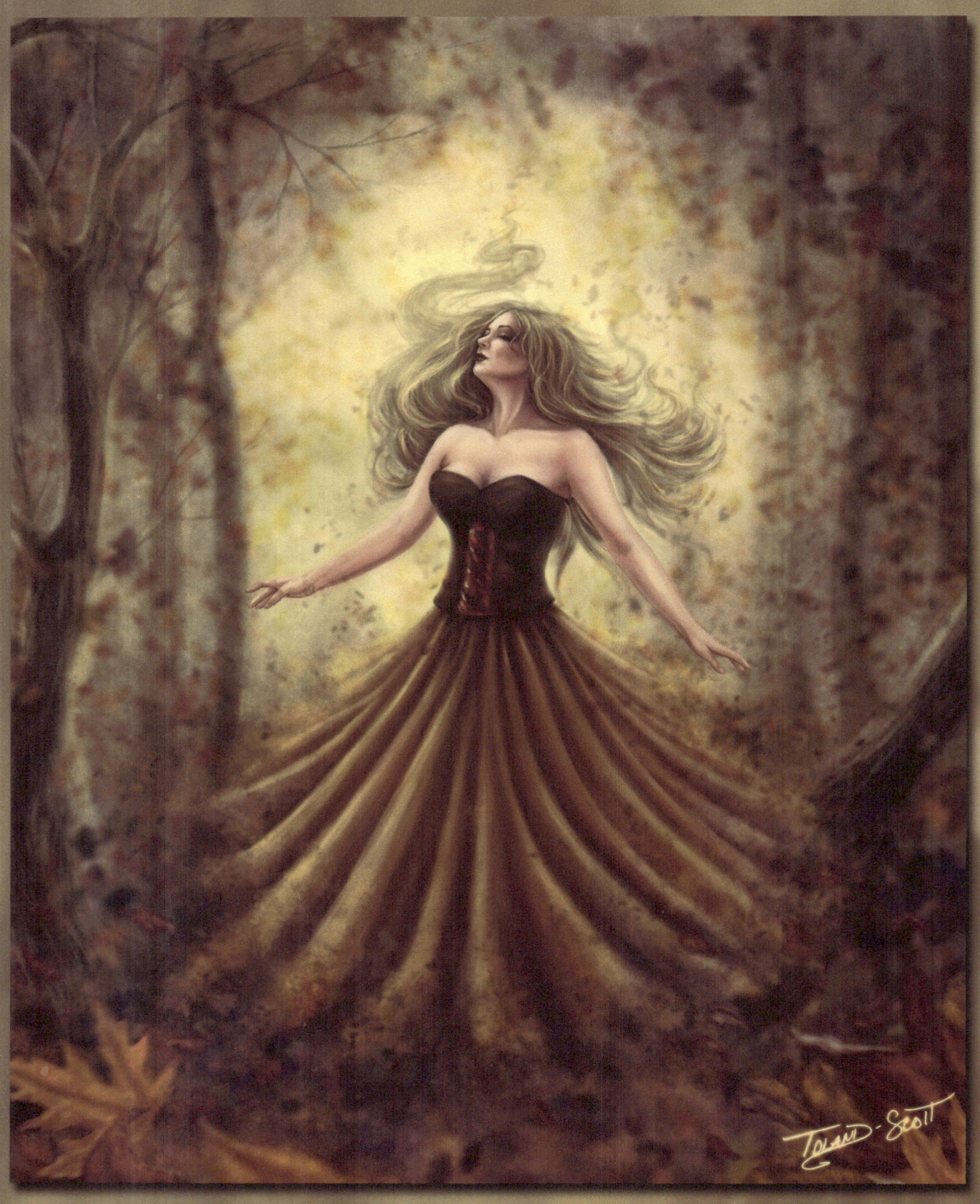

"Breath of Autumn", 2012

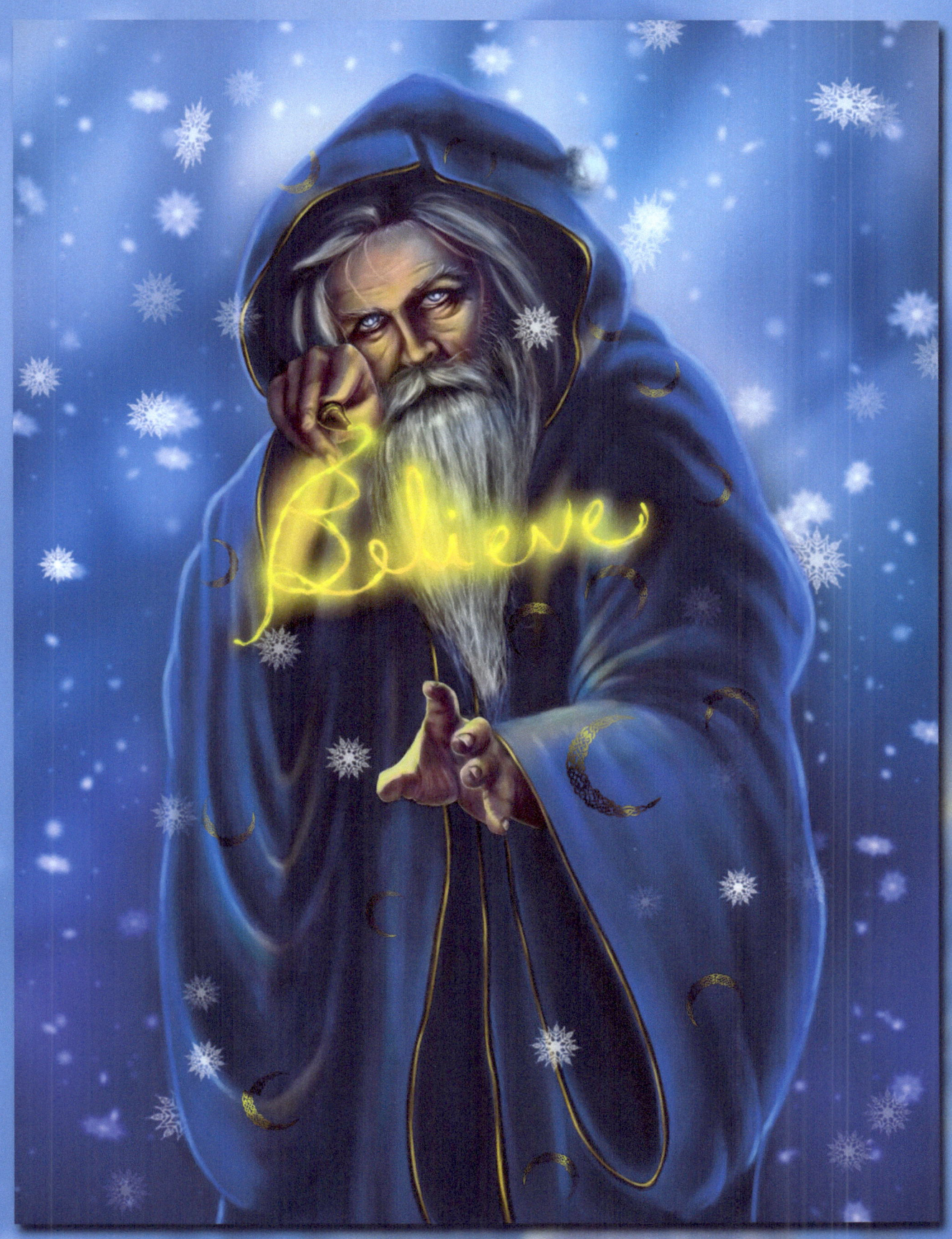

"Believe", 2009

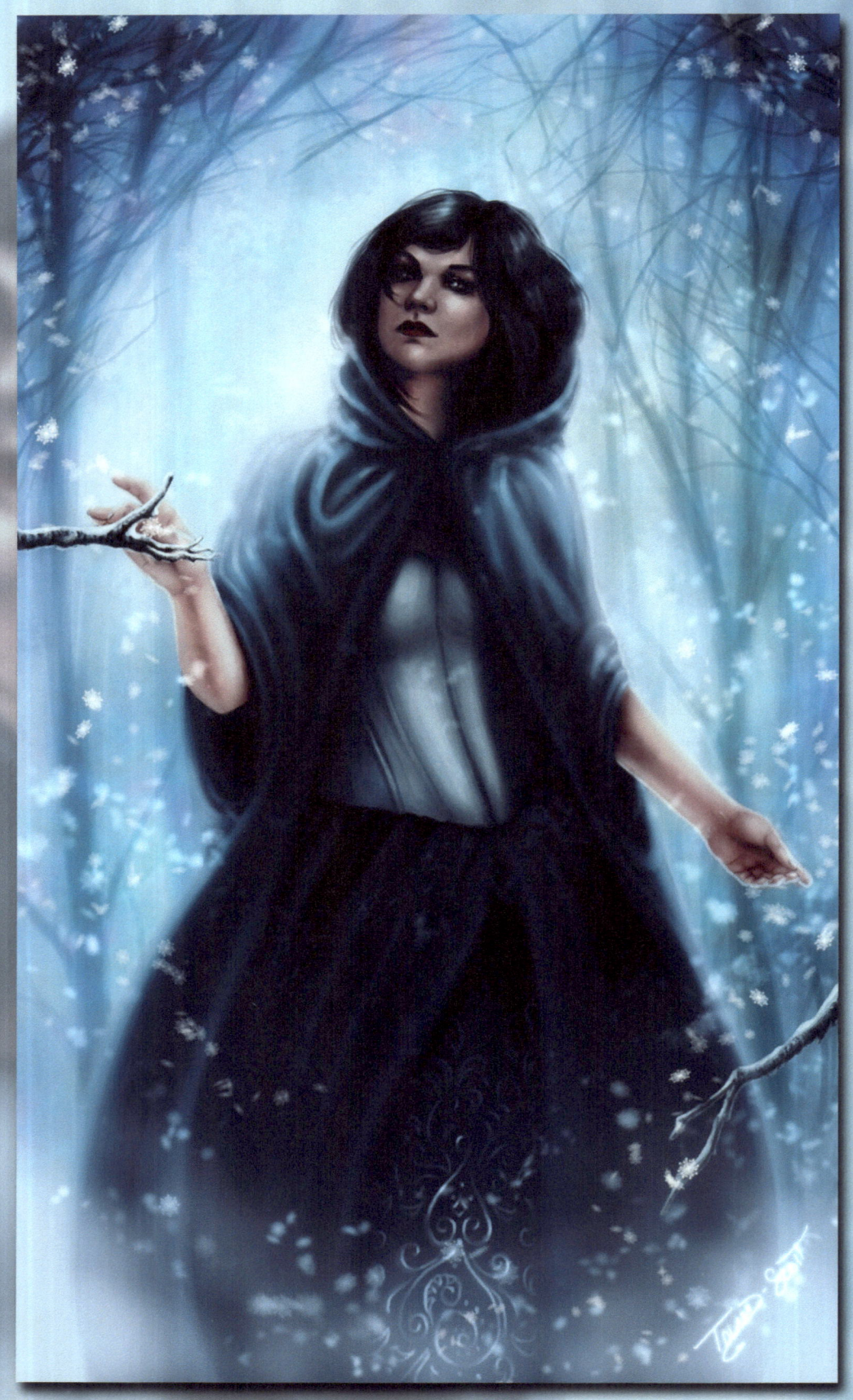

"Winter Spirit", 2012

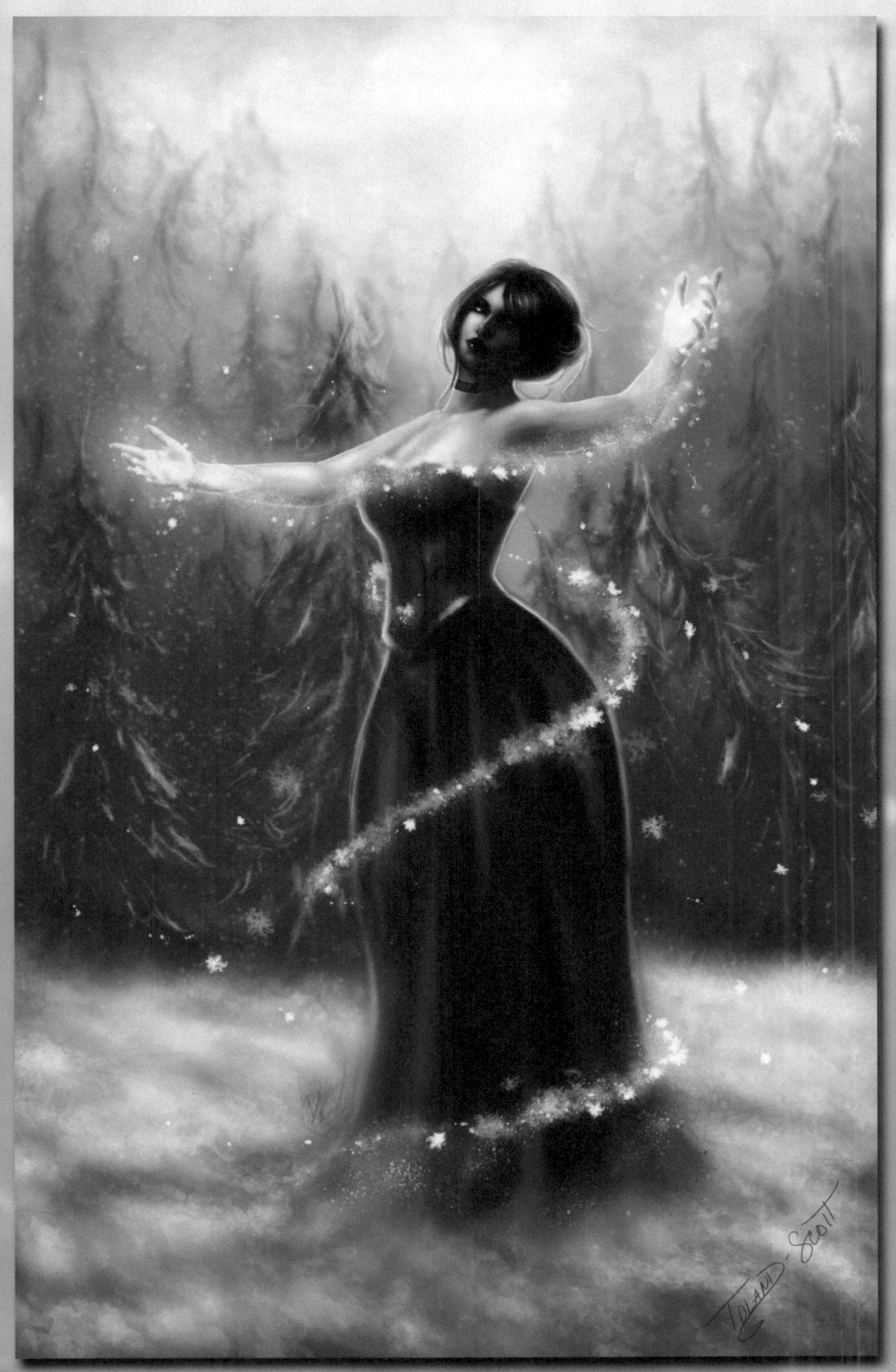

"Frost", 2011

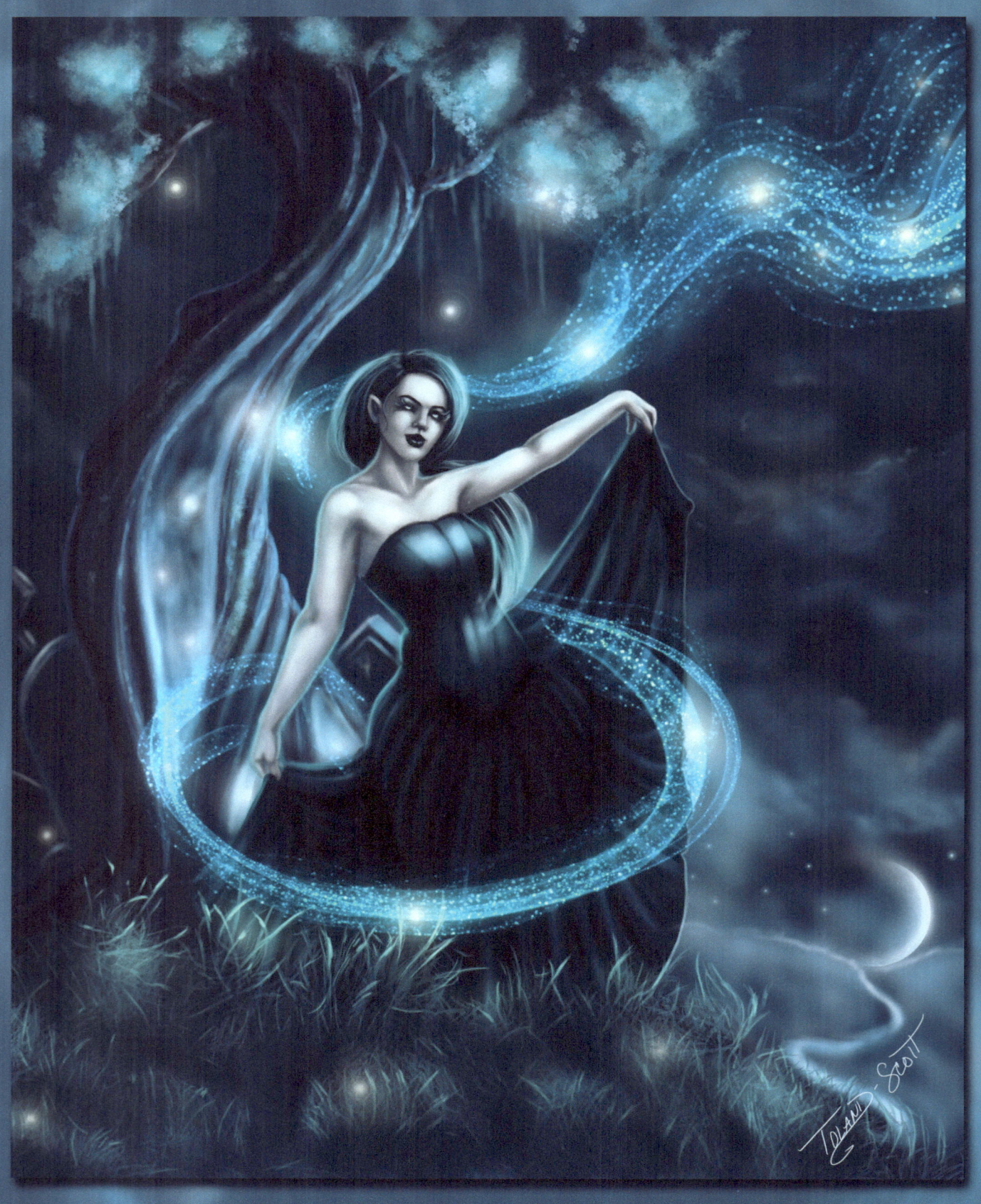

"Harmony of Night", 2012

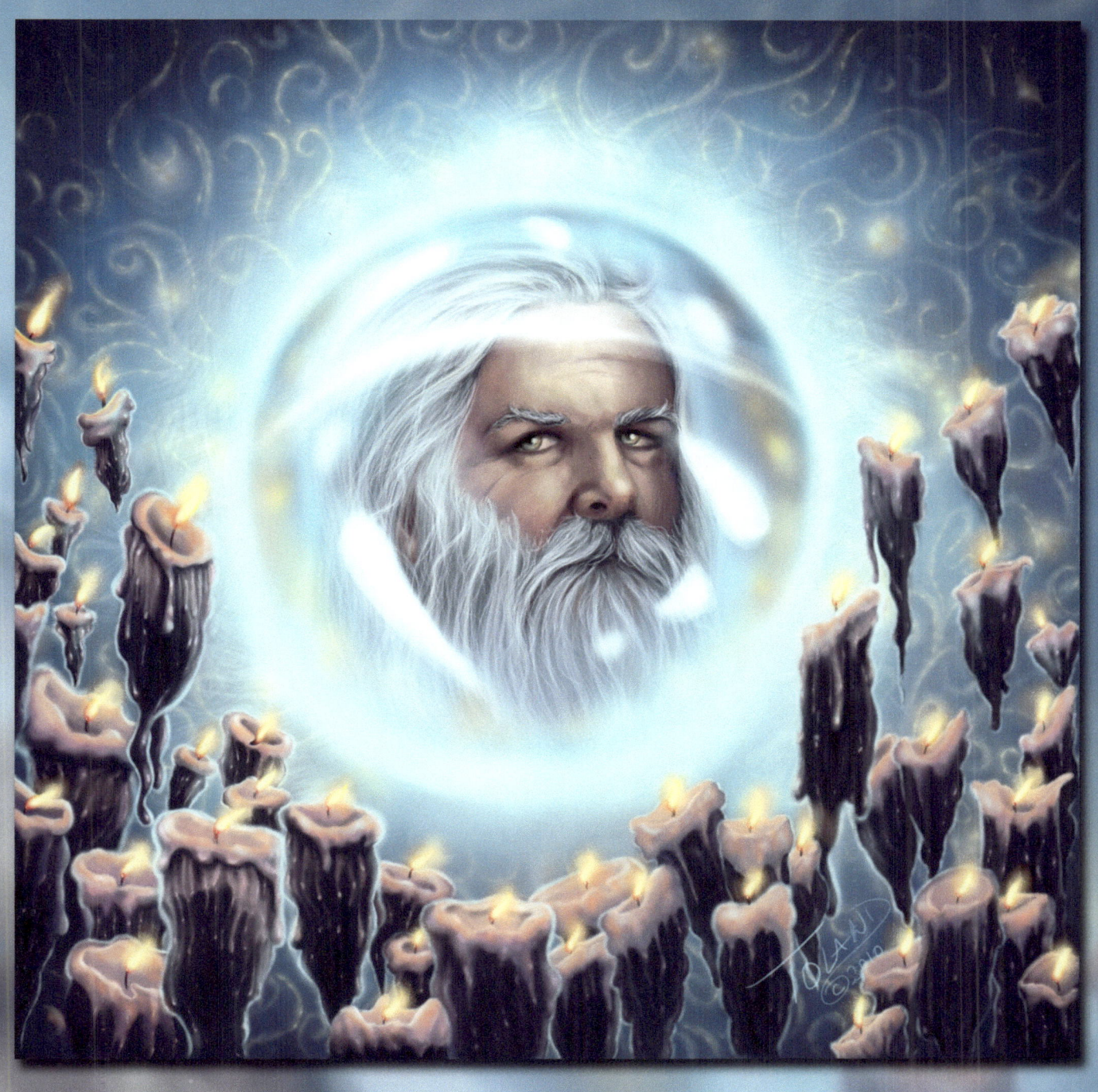

"Locked Within the Crystal Ball", 2010

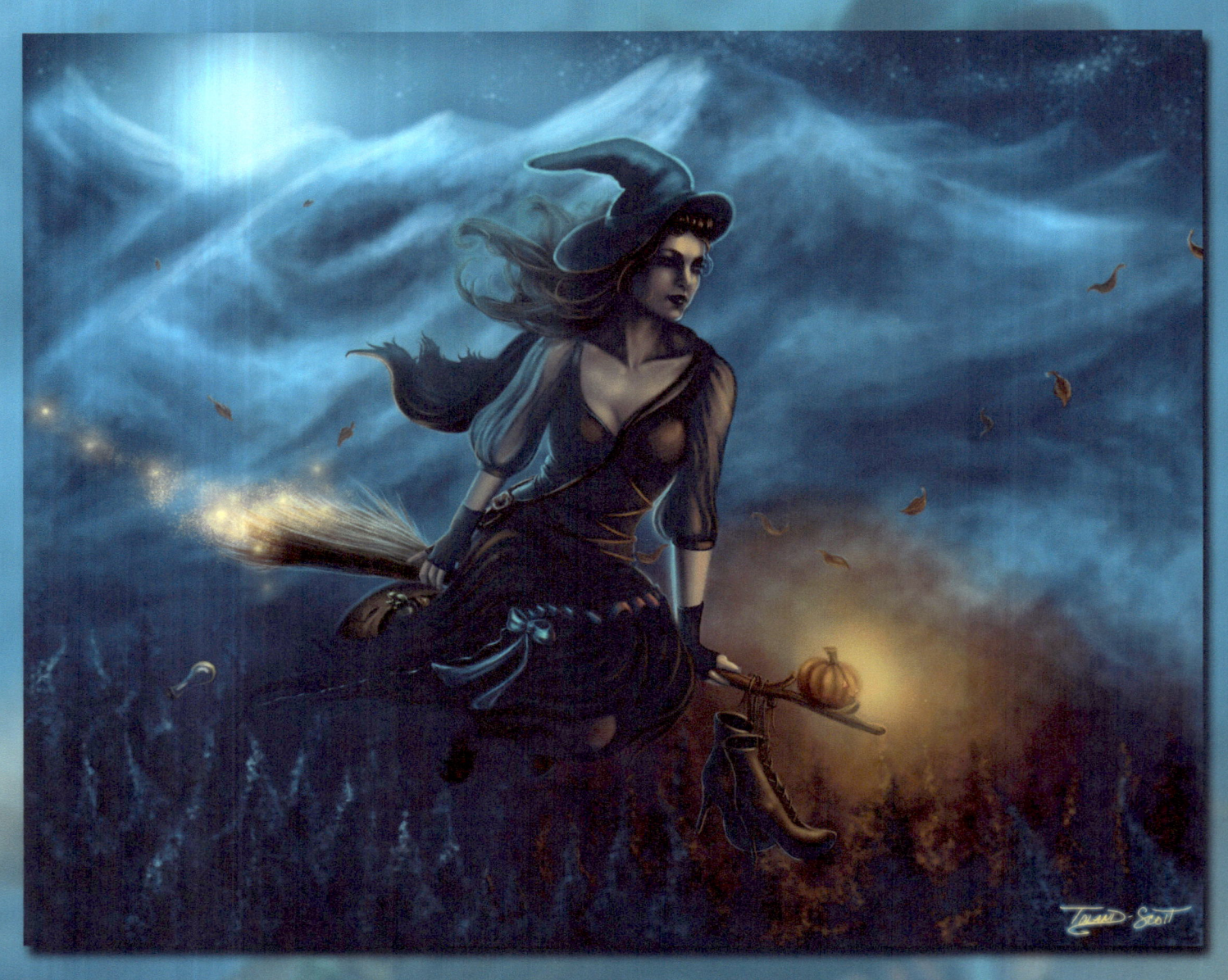

"Midnight Errands", 2012

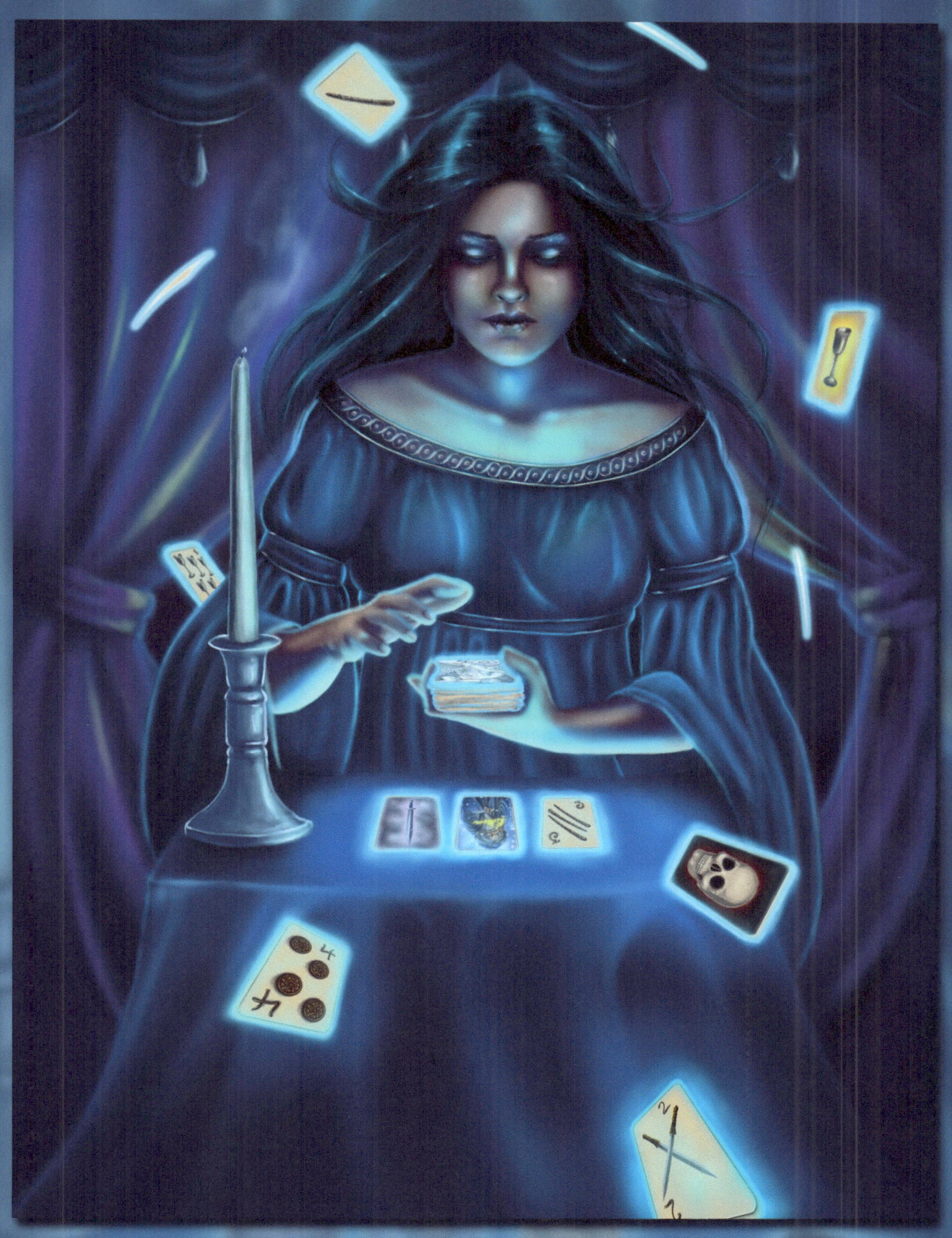

"Mirrors of Time", 2009

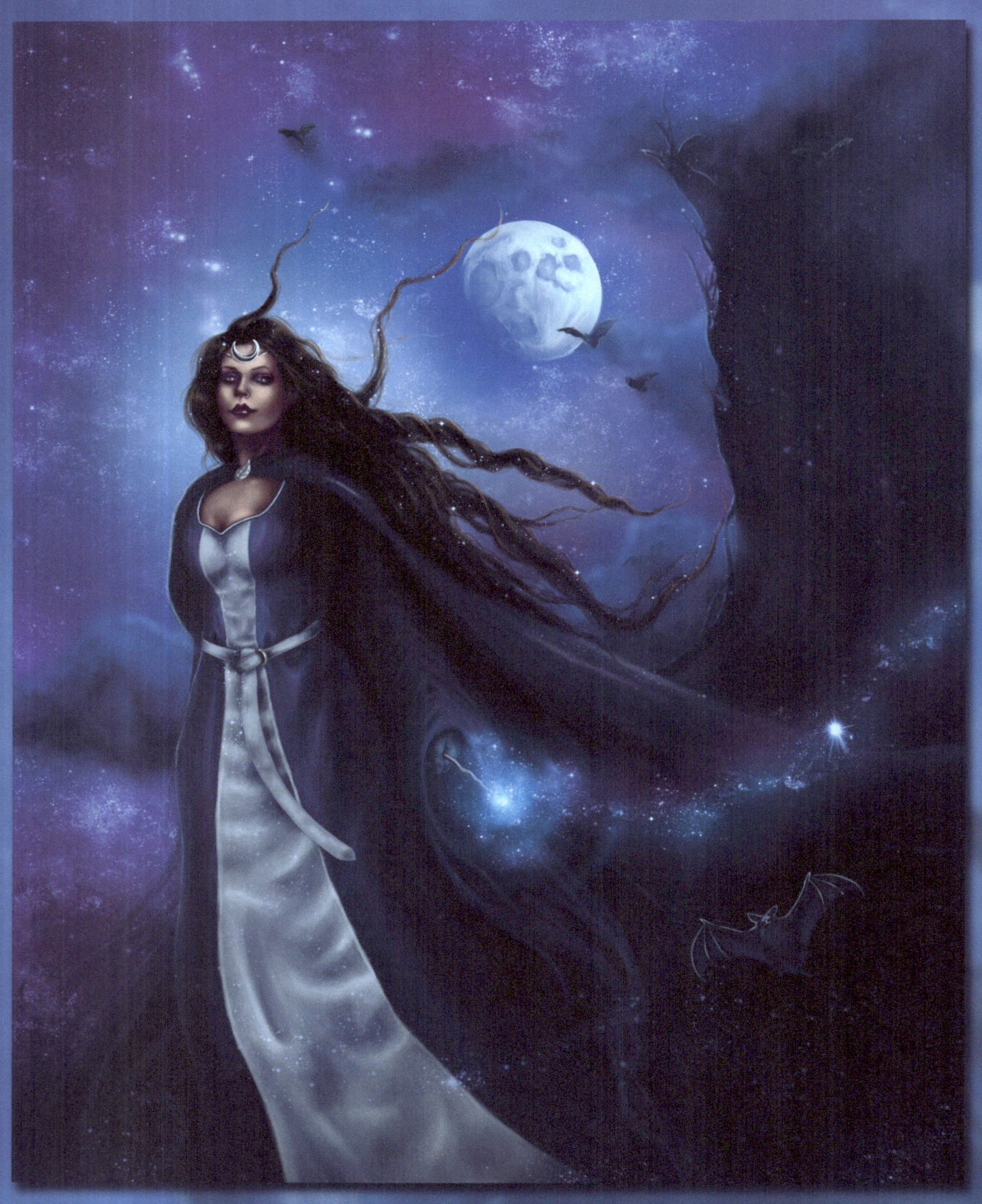

"Nyx", 2009

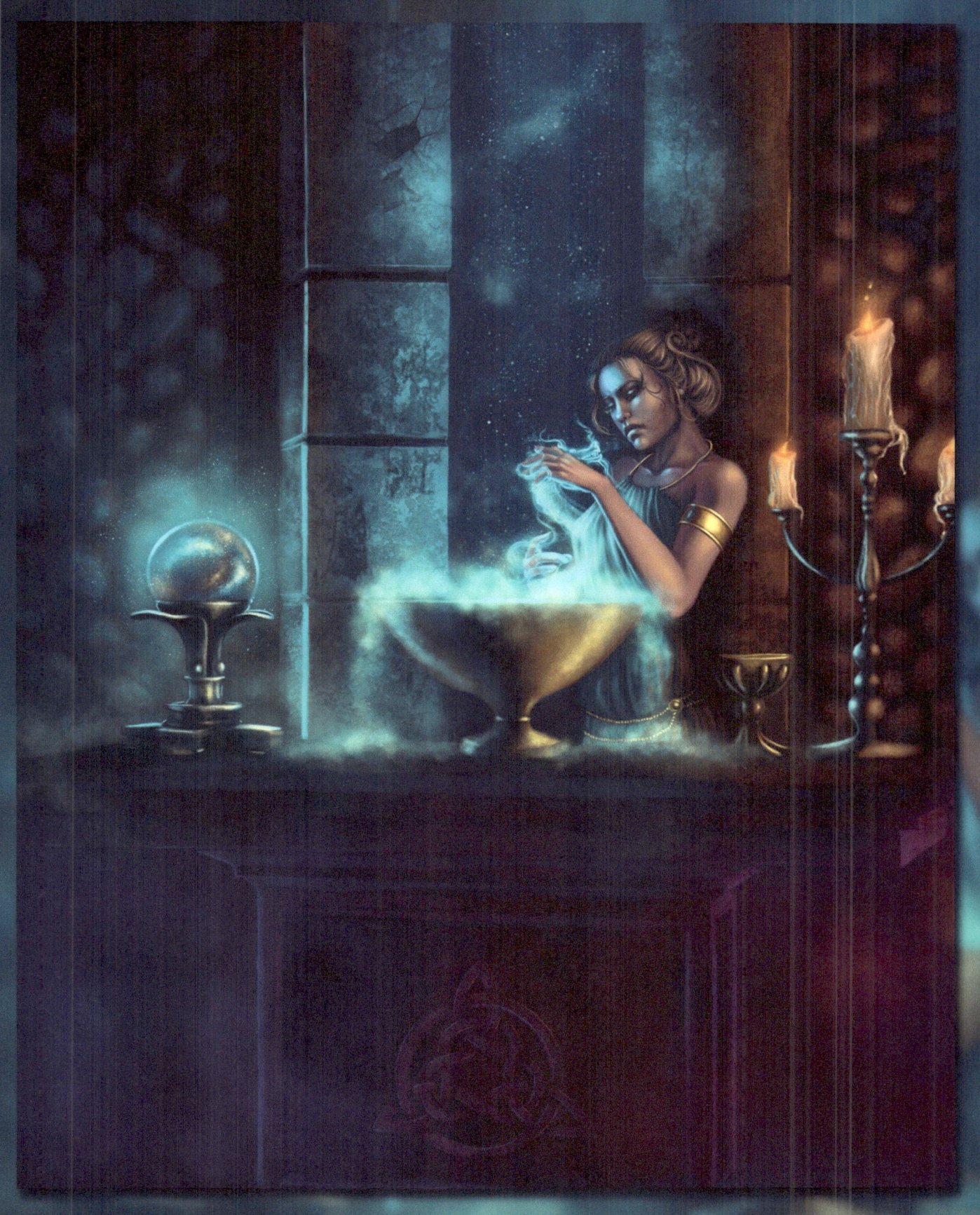

"Phantasmal Familiar", 2012

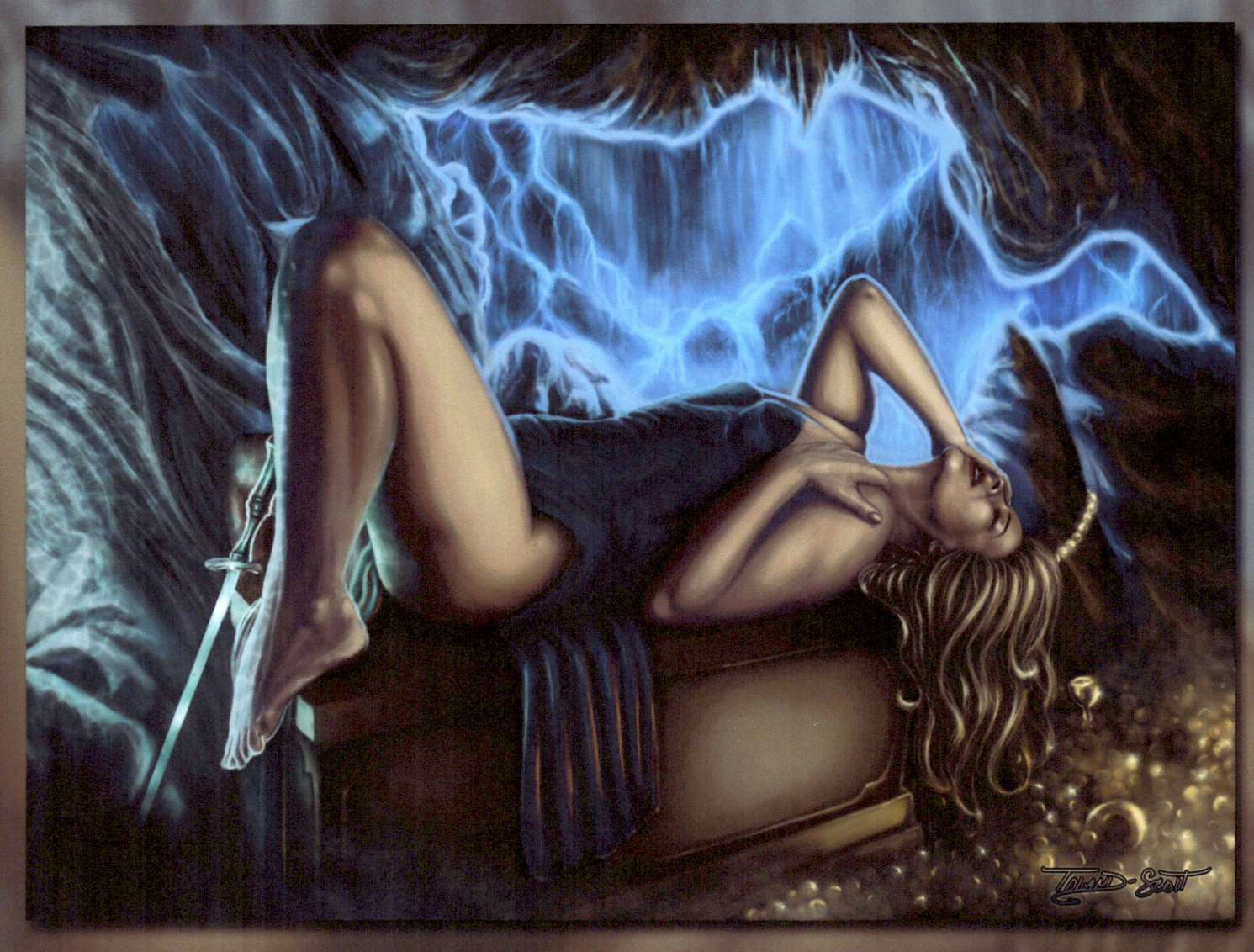

"Small Sacrifice", 2012

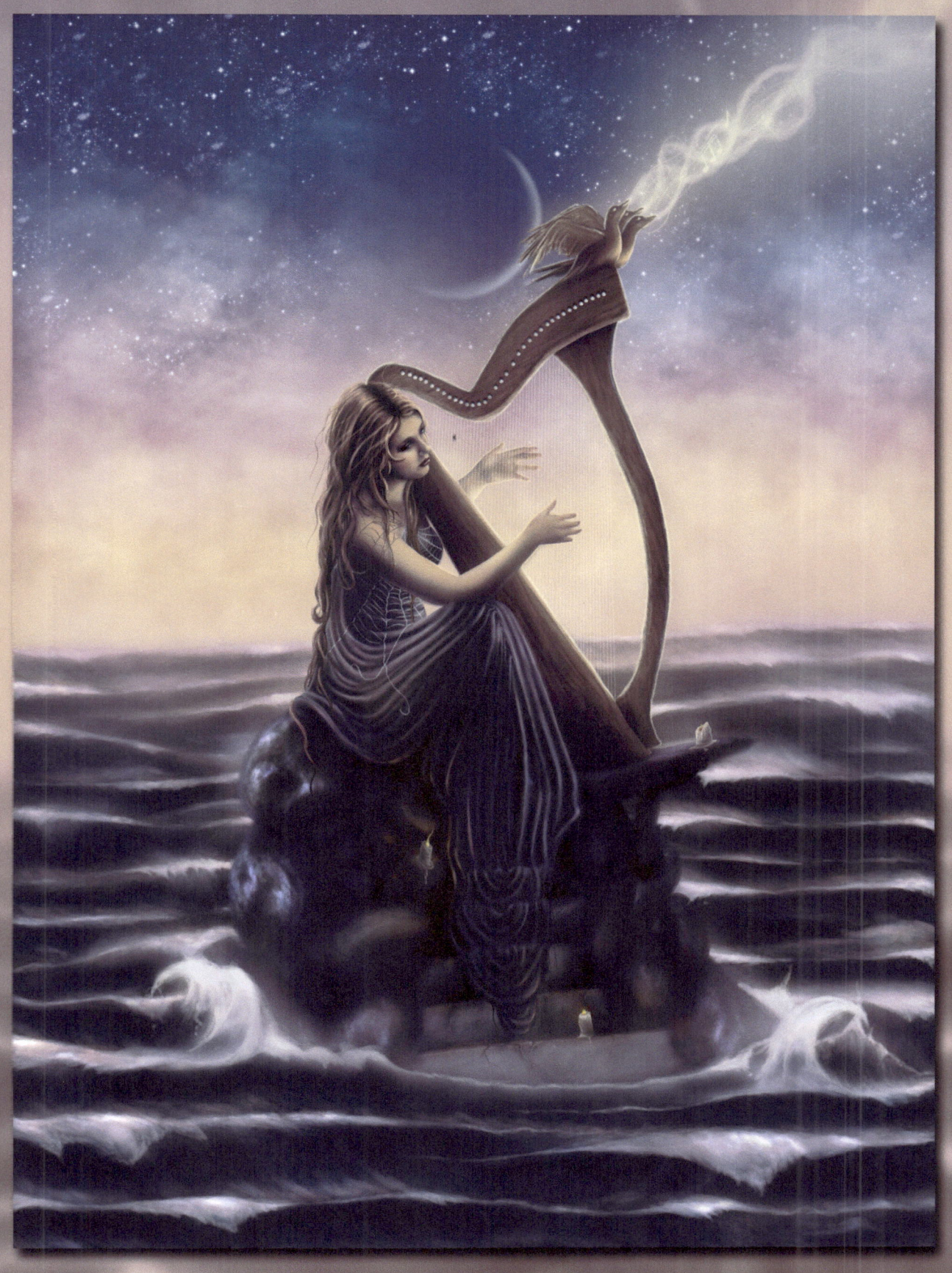

"Moon's Song", 2009

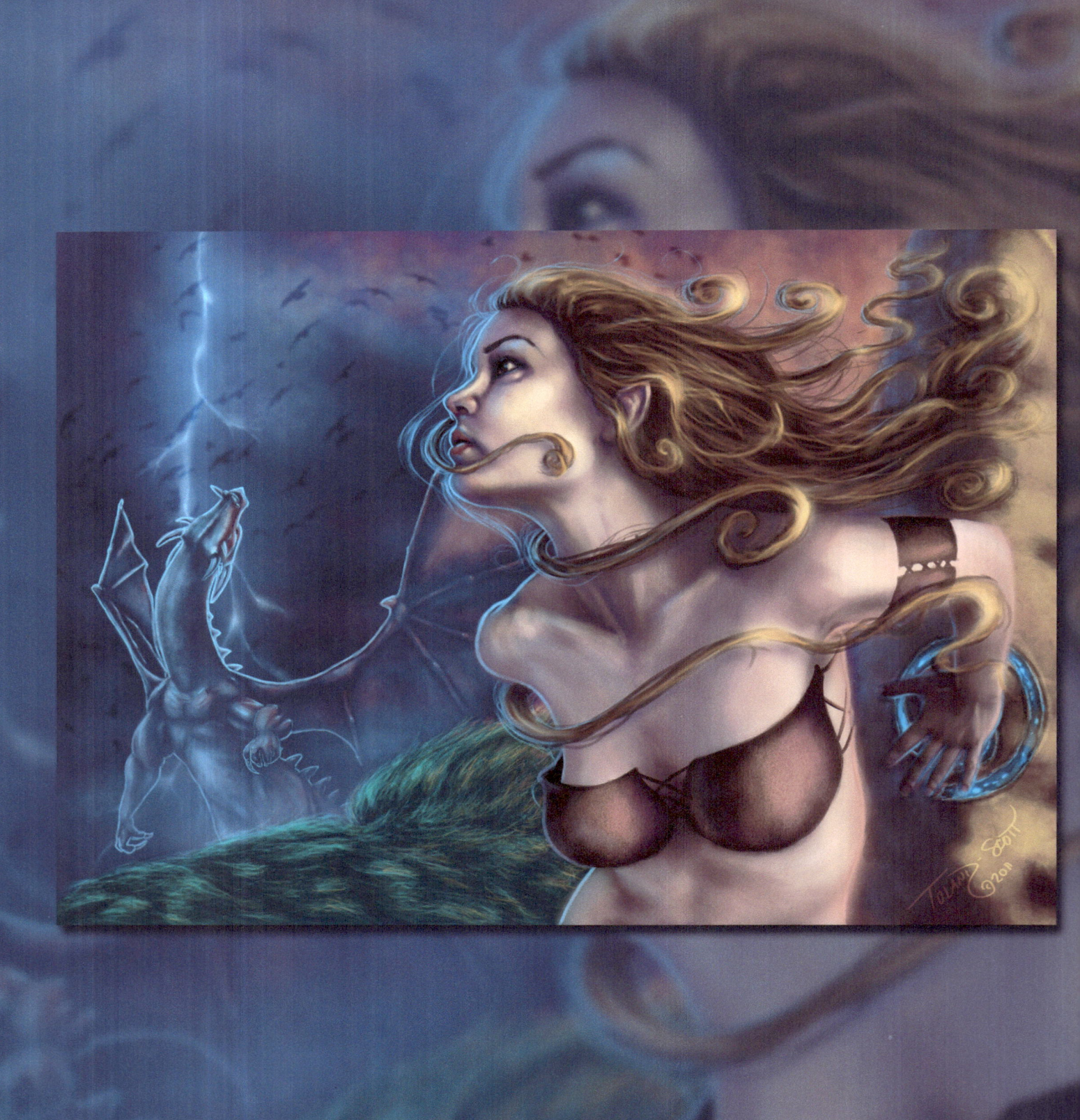

"Skies of Fire", 2011

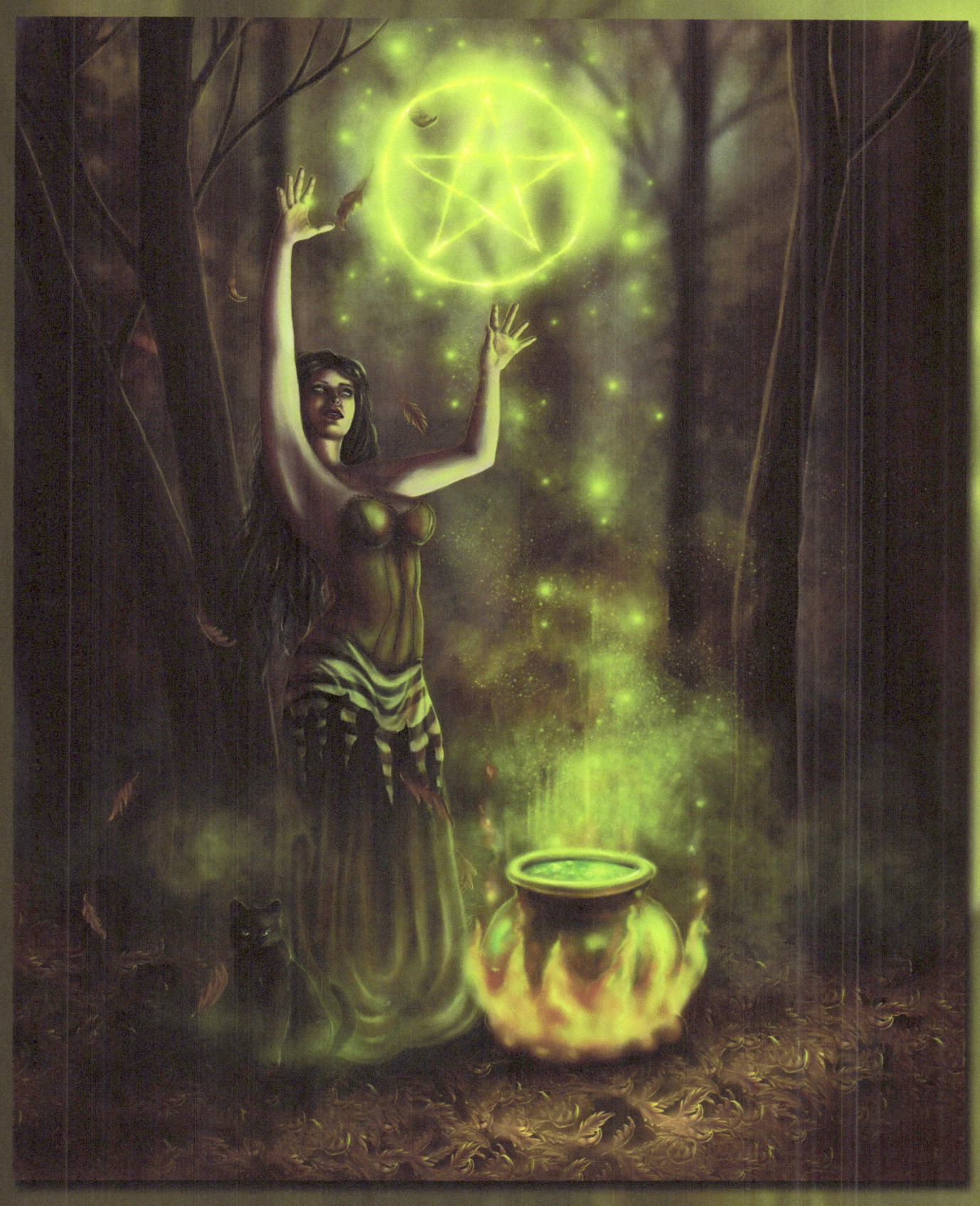

"Spirit of Samhain", 2009

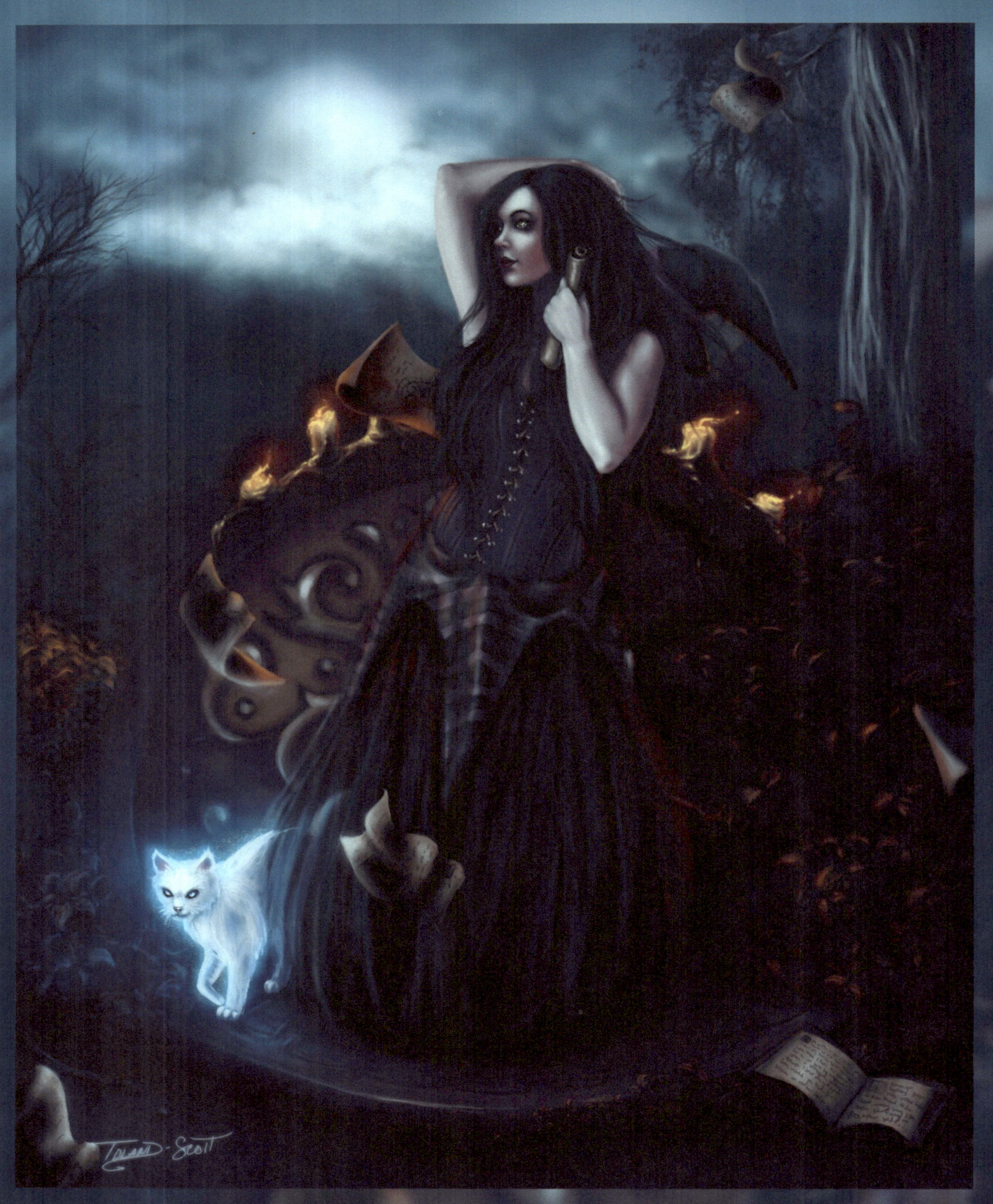

"The Witching Hour", 2012

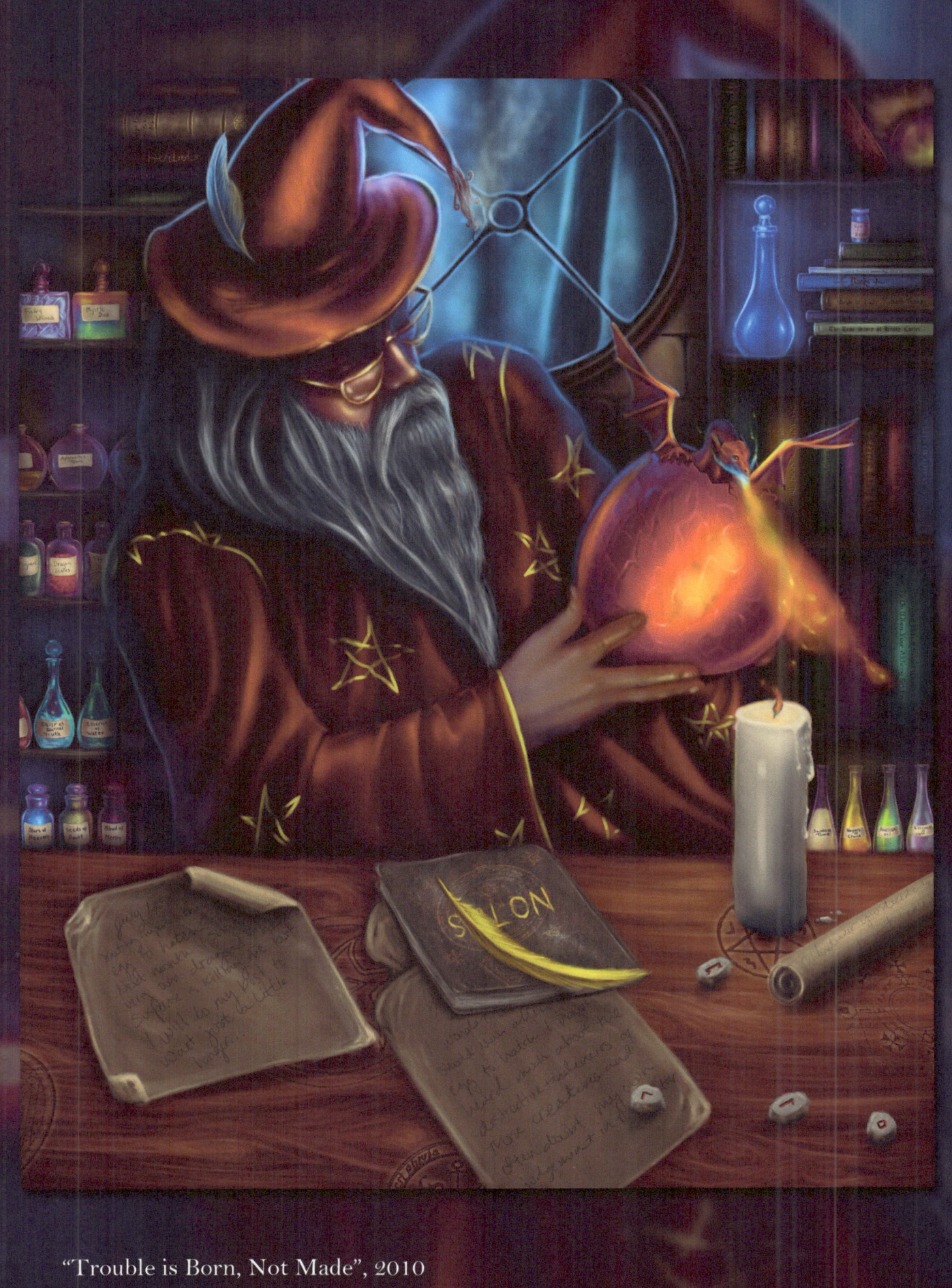

"Trouble is Born, Not Made", 2010

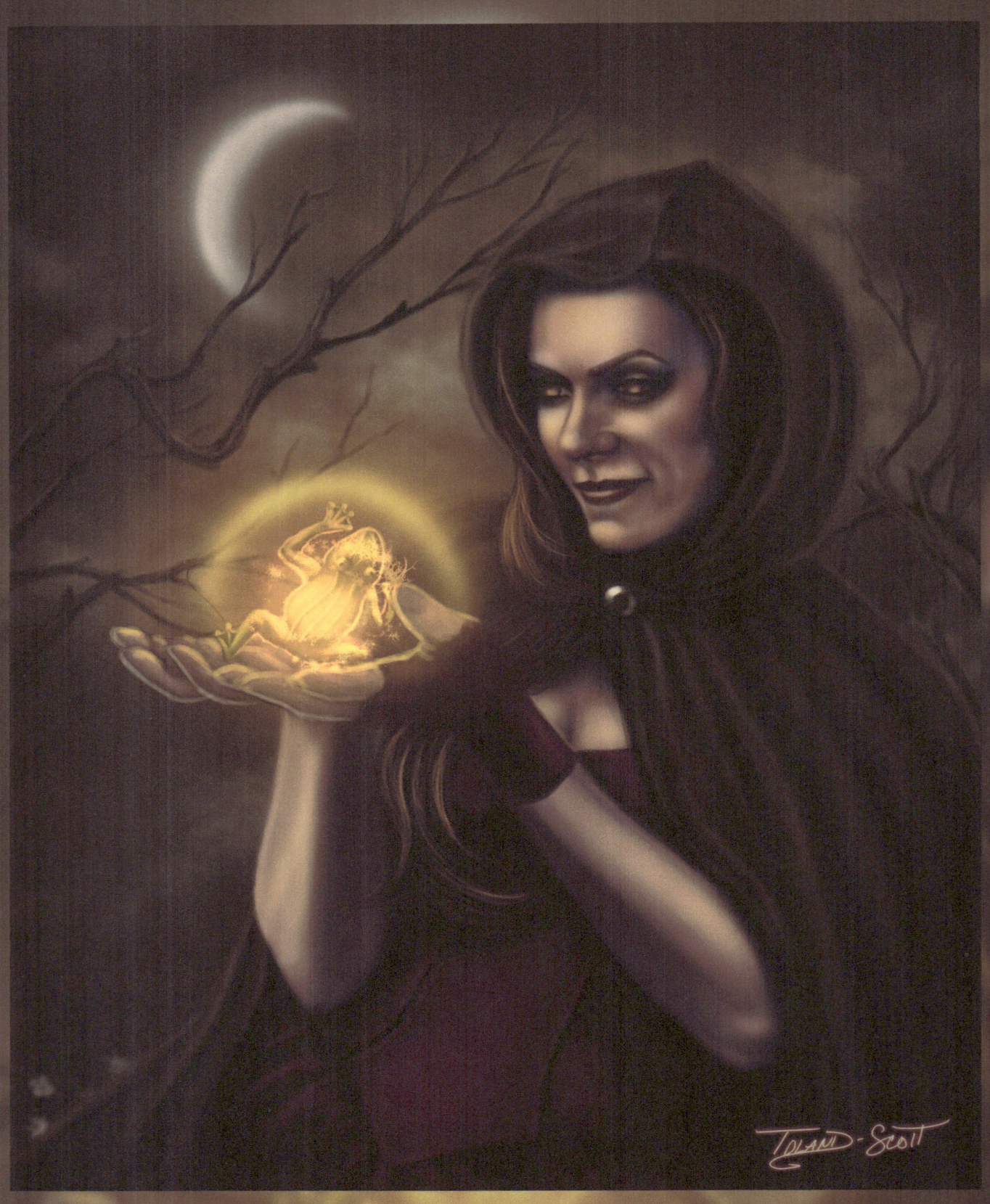

"Toadification", 2012

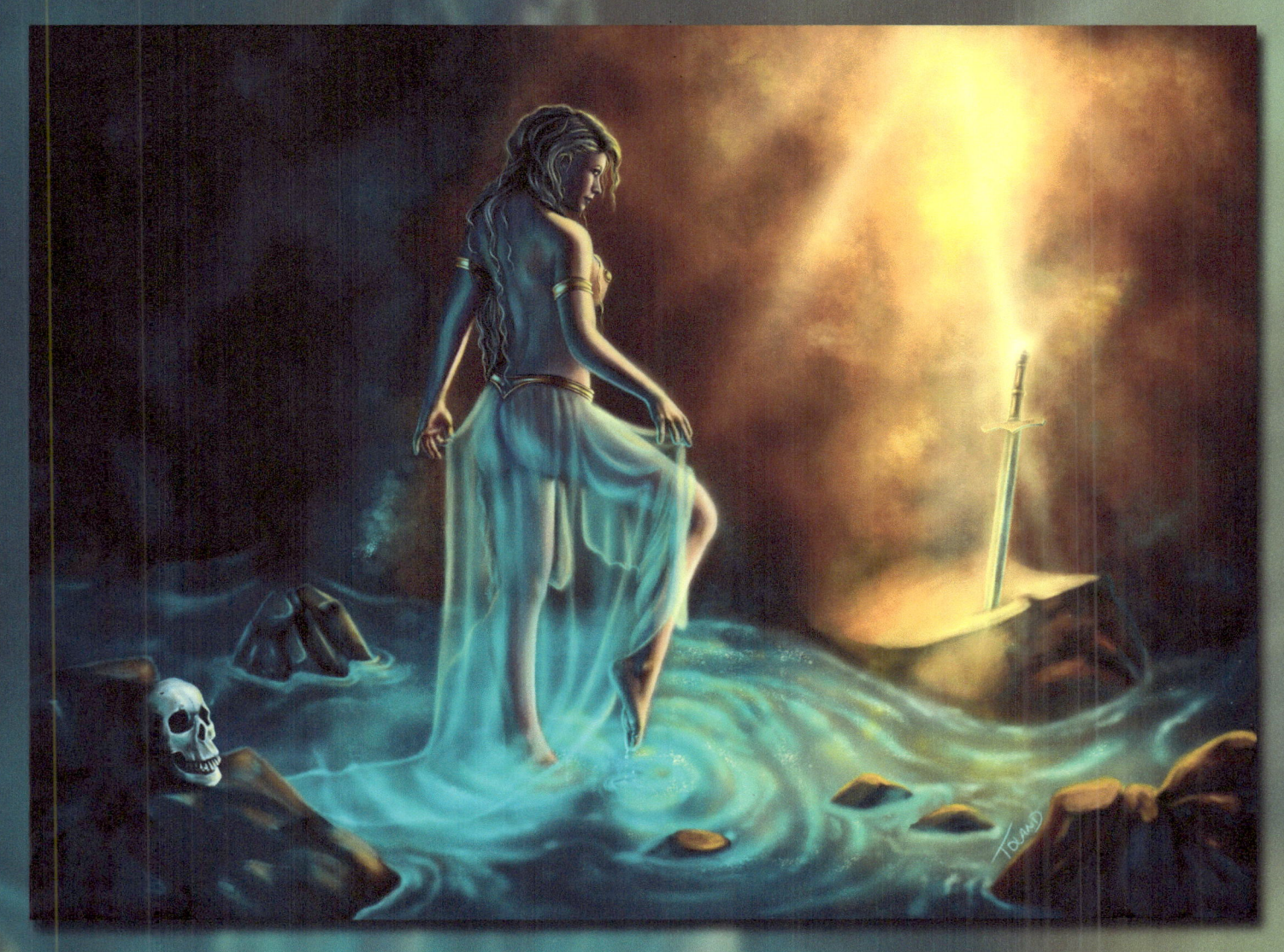

"Unlikely Guardian", 2010

I hope you have enjoyed this foray into my imagination.
It has truly been an honor to share my artwork with you, whether in this book, in person, or via the Internet.
I hope someday soon to publish a final installment of digital art before I begin to compile my new oil paintings into a similar collection. Your support brings these dreams closer and closer every day.

Thank you!